# SUCCE$$
## Demands a Master Plan

**MIKE INGRAM**

Copyright © 2025 by Mike Ingram

# SUCCE$$
### Demands a Master Plan

All rights reserved. No part of this publication may be reproduced, distributed, or transmitted in any form or by any means, including photocopying, recording, or other electronic or mechanical methods, without the prior written permission of the publisher, except in the case of brief quotations embodied in critical reviews and certain other noncommercial uses permitted by copyright law.

For permission requests, write to the publisher, addressed
"Attention: Permissions Coordinator,"
reception@markvictorhansenlibrary.com

Quantity sales special discounts are available on quantity purchases by corporations, associations, and others. For details, contact the publisher at reception@markvictorhansenlibrary.com

Orders by U.S. trade bookstores and wholesalers.
Email: reception@markvictorhansenlibrary.com

Creative Contributions - Veronica Deisler and Carol McManus
Book Layout & Cover Design - DBree

Manufactured and printed in the United States of America distributed globally by markvictorhansenlibrary.com

**MVHL**

New York | Los Angeles | London | Sydney

ISBN: 979-8-88581-232-0 Hardback
ISBN: 979-8-88581-233-7 Paperback
ISBN: 979-8-88581-199-6 eBook
Library of Congress Control Number: 2025911561

SUCCE$$ DEMANDS A MASTER PLAN

My dear mother, Maude Ingram.

# DEDICATION

*To my mother, C. Maude Ingram,
who gave in every way.*

My dad, Paul Ingram, was a godly and good man. In the thirteen years I had with him, we shared plenty of special father-and-son experiences I will never forget. He took me to many ball games and taught me how to hunt and fish. Unfortunately, he died when he was only forty-two years old, after battling cancer for three years.

My mom was only thirty-six years old when she found herself a frightened widow with a thirteen-year-old son trying to find his place in life. She was also uneducated and faced a huge mortgage on the motel my dad had built, as well as stacks of medical and hospital bills.

**Mom with a few of her close friends for her 85th birthday party.**

## Dedication

My mom may have been uneducated, but she was strong and held on to the memory of my father. She never remarried or even dated another man. She was concerned that another man might not treat me with the same love and affection my father had. "No one can match your dad," she told me.

She also knew how to pray, and prayer was required at every meal and at bedtime. We were in church whenever the church door was open. I never tried to test her will, and I honored and accepted her faith and values. My mom endured more heartache and pain than anyone I know. She was truly a saint. All I can say is, "Thanks, Mom."

In fact, it was my mom's love and Christian example that helped shape my appreciation for the other important women in my life. I owe the women who've supported me along the way for the success I've had. My wife, Sheila, has been with me every step of the way. She keeps my perspective about family, faith, and business real. Deb Bricker has been on my longest business journey from the beginning. She's the foundational strength for me and for all who work with me. Denise Organ is always at my side. She anticipates and resolves our needs before we know we have them.

There are so many other incredible women in my life, whether they are in our office, among our investors, or through our philanthropic endeavors. Without them, we would not have realized or enjoyed our Master Plan.

# TABLE OF CONTENTS

Dedication . . . . . . . . . . . . . . . . . . . . . . . . . . . . . . . . . vii
Foreword By Zig Ziglar (from the First Edition, 2012). . . 1
Introduction. . . . . . . . . . . . . . . . . . . . . . . . . . . . . . . . .5
Background . . . . . . . . . . . . . . . . . . . . . . . . . . . . . . . .9

THE FIRST KEY: PEOPLE POWER . . . . . . . . . . . . . . . .21
  1   The Power Of Relationships . . . . . . . . . . . . . . . . . . .23
  2   The Power Of Networking. . . . . . . . . . . . . . . . . . . .43
  3   The Power Of Partnerships . . . . . . . . . . . . . . . . . . 55
  4   The Power Of Teamwork . . . . . . . . . . . . . . . . . . . .65
  5   The Power Of Loyalty . . . . . . . . . . . . . . . . . . . . . . .77
  6   The Power Of Trust . . . . . . . . . . . . . . . . . . . . . . . . .83
  7   The Power Of Customers. . . . . . . . . . . . . . . . . . . . .93

THE SECOND KEY: PRODUCT POWER. . . . . . . . . . . .97
  8   The Power Of Innovation. . . . . . . . . . . . . . . . . . . . .99
  9   The Power Of Design . . . . . . . . . . . . . . . . . . . . . . .109
 10   The Power Of Adding Value . . . . . . . . . . . . . . . . . .117
 11   The Power Of Creative Marketing. . . . . . . . . . . . . .123
 12   The Power Of Service . . . . . . . . . . . . . . . . . . . . . .141
 13   The Power Of Thinking Big . . . . . . . . . . . . . . . . . .147
 14   The Power Of The Multiple Win. . . . . . . . . . . . . . .161

THE THIRD KEY: PERSONAL POWER . . . . . . . . . . . .167
 15   The Power Of Vision . . . . . . . . . . . . . . . . . . . . . . .169
 16   The Power Of Enthusiasm. . . . . . . . . . . . . . . . . . . .185
 17   The Power Of Integrity. . . . . . . . . . . . . . . . . . . . . .191
 18   The Power Of Forgiveness. . . . . . . . . . . . . . . . . . . .199
 19   The Power Of Persistence . . . . . . . . . . . . . . . . . . . .205

| 20 | The Power Of Giving Back................221 |
|---|---|
| 21 | The Power Of Mentoring..................243 |
| 22 | The Power Of Freedom...................251 |

Epilogue: El Dorado Holdings Today...............259
In Summary: The Ultimate Master Plan............267
A Postscript........................................271
Acknowledgments................................275
About the Author Mike Ingram ..................279
The Horatio Alger Association ....................283

# FOREWORD
## from Zig Ziglar

I've always believed—and told anyone who would listen to me—that success is 90% attitude, and 10% other stuff. Then I met Mike Ingram. Mike is all about attitude, attitude, attitude. The "other stuff" barely comes in second.

Mike Ingram didn't become one of the most successful men I've ever met because of what he has accomplished. His success lies in his attitudes.

He has the right attitude about people. He knows that by building relationships, he can build a successful business and a successful life. He knows that by helping others succeed—employees, investors, and clients—everyone becomes a winner. Mike does not believe in *either/or*. He believes in *all*.

He has the right attitude about his product. He realizes that a successful business cannot sacrifice quality on the altar of immediate sales or short-term profit. His product is all about long-term results—satisfied investors, development partners, and customers.

He has the right attitude about power. He understands that power isn't about control. Power comes from the values that empower the individual. He understands that true power springs forth from integrity, compassion, and sacrifice for others.

## Foreword from Zig Ziglar

Right now, you might be thinking that a man such as Mike Ingram couldn't possibly be real. That he couldn't actually exist.

Good news, friend. He is real! He does exist!! I know because I count him among my closest friends. He would probably tell you that I am his mentor and he is my protégé. But I see just the opposite. In many respects, Mike is my mentor and I am his protégé.

Knowledge is as individual as we are. No one can learn it all, apply it all, or teach it all. The same thing applies to wisdom. No one is *all wise*. Yet, great knowledge and wisdom are available to you through the pages of this book.

Mike has used proven, time-honored techniques to build, expand, and enjoy his business and his life. He has learned how to develop a loyal customer base, how to add significant value to products and services, and how to regroup after devastating setbacks. This is a story of overcoming, whether it was surviving tough economic times or forgiving those who sought to take advantage of him. It's about following a well-designed "Master Plan." At his core, Mike Ingram is also a Christian businessman. He has lost or gained more wealth than most of us will ever see. But through his experiences, he has learned to trust God. Faith is the foundation upon which his businesses have been built. You will learn valuable business principles from his life; principles that will guide you or strengthen you when you face the lions of adversity.

This book is a special gift to you by an amazing, caring leader who has experienced the valleys and the peaks of building a business. It's destined to become a classic book of encouragement for all who want to launch or rebuild their own businesses—or discover or recapture the greatness in their lives.

**—Zig Ziglar**
May 2012, Dallas, Texas
(from the First Edition of this book)

Zig Ziglar died on November 28, 2012, leaving an incredible library and legacy of wisdom that lives on through everyone whose lives he touched. It was an honor to have his friendship and mentorship.

# INTRODUCTION

Starting and operating a successful business is just about the toughest pursuit there is in life. In fact, I can only think of one more difficult—starting and maintaining a successful marriage!

The fact is that business and marriage have several things in common. They both require a Master Plan. They both are built on vision, commitment, and integrity. But it goes beyond that. In both business and marriage, *creativity* is essential.

Vision empowers you, your business, and your partner to set a specific goal, determine your intended direction, and work toward it. Commitment is the driving force that helps you move in your intended direction to achieve your goal. Integrity is what holds it all together.

But creativity? Well, that's the *secret sauce*. It's the spice in marriage. And it's the recipe for success in business.

Creativity is what confounds your competitors, pleases your customers, amazes your investors, and inspires your team. It can take many forms and be operative in many areas of a business. It can be expressed in your product or service itself, in the way you market your product or service, and in the way you serve customers. I would venture to say that creativity is even at the foundation of loyalty—on the part of all your key constituents, including your customers, your suppliers, your investors, and your team.

## Introduction

A perfect example of the role of creativity can be seen in the late Steve Jobs of Apple Inc. Although you could argue that some of his tactics were less than admirable (read one of his biographies to see what I mean), I've seldom seen a leader who inspires such dedication in his team or such admiration and loyalty from his customers. Apple people could be described as fanatics, and not necessarily in a negative way. Who other than an Apple customer would line up outside an Apple Store hours before the release of a new iPhone or iPad? The phenomenon is largely due to Apple's unswerving devotion to creativity in everything they offer. Their products are beautifully designed, easy to use, and they perform as promised.

I admit I'm no Steve Jobs, although there is one similarity between Apple and my company. Just as throngs of people get in line for Apple's latest offerings, our investors line up in eager anticipation of our latest offerings. Here's an example: We used to send our proposals on new investments to our prospects via FedEx, but our investors on the West Coast complained. They said the East Coast investors had a three-hour advantage, based on time-zone differences. Our new programs would be sold out before people in California, Nevada, Oregon, and Washington had an opportunity to review the offers. We've since solved the issue by telling prospective investors in advance when new projects will be announced. Then we announce them via email so they all have an equal opportunity.

I believe we've achieved success because, long before I heard of Steve Jobs, I took a look at successful individuals and companies and determined why they were successful. I learned that they focused on three key areas that gave them an edge. They became the components of my own Master Plan. These key areas are:

1. People Power
2. Product Power
3. Personal Power

As you read this book, you may say to yourself, "These ideas are so simple, I could have thought of them." I'm sure you could have. So, what makes this book significant and valuable to you? It's the way these principles work together as a whole. These are life principles, not just business principles. In other words, as you begin to apply these principles to your life as well as to your business, your success in both life and in business will be more meaningful to you.

There's one more component to these principles that guides my own life and business. That is my faith and trust in God. It helps me to understand these principles better and to use them as building blocks for a better life and business. Whether or not you share my beliefs, these principles will guide you in a positive way toward success.

There are no shortcuts to success. It begins with a vision, a willing commitment to a plan, and a plan that is filled with integrity. You are the creator of your own plan. You have your own vision, and you need to work your own plan with integrity. And just don't forget to throw in a little creativity for the fun of it!

Join me on a journey that is sure to bring a unique Master Plan to your life!

# BACKGROUND

Now, the question in the back of your mind—or maybe even in the front of your mind—may be, "Who is Mike Ingram and why should I care what he has to say?"

I think that's a valid question. When I read a book (and I read lots of them), I usually know something about the writer or the person whose story is the focus of the book. If I want to learn more about a certain subject, I don't need to know about the writer. For example, I love stories about the history of the Old West. If a friend with the same interest recommends a book, I don't care who the author is—I read it.

But in the case of this book, I'm both the author and the subject. I'm sharing my life with readers who know nothing about me.

So, why then, should you care?

Before I answer your question, I want to make it clear that I'm not writing this book so you'll think I'm some "big deal." I'm not the world's greatest anything. Not the world's greatest husband, father, or friend. Not the world's greatest boss or businessman. Not even the world's best example of the points I want to illustrate.

I'm writing this book to give you a gift. That gift is my insight into what makes for a rewarding, fulfilling life. I'm here to say, "If you focus on these three simple principles in

# Background

your daily life, there's no goal you can't reach . . . no dream you can't achieve."

I'm proof of that, and that's why you should care.

My personal story is like most everyone else's. It's filled with ups and downs, successes and failures, joys and sorrows, and all the other things that make up the complex mixture we call "our lives."

I'm the product of a small-town upbringing. I worked several jobs throughout junior high and high school. I was a freshman at Pasadena Nazarene College (now known as Point Loma Nazarene University) in California. I went there because I was recruited for a swim team that never actually materialized. About the only thing I took seriously my freshman year was the National Hot Rod Association (NHRA) drag racing.

When the dean of the college, a wonderful man named Paul Culbertson, invited me into his office, he strongly suggested I continue my education somewhere else. Based on my aptitude testing, he steered me toward an agribusiness degree. My aptitude test indicated a strong interest in both agriculture and business. It occurred to me I should probably get serious about my education, too, and I transferred to Texas Tech. Somewhere along the line, it also dawned on me that people with better grade point averages were probably going to get better job offers and make more money.

From that point on, I worked hard to raise my lowly 2.0 GPA, and I continued to apply myself for the rest of my college years. I eventually graduated from The University of New Mexico in May 1966 with a Bachelor of Science in

## Background

Agriculture and was named to the Alpha Zeta National Honor Fraternity (now Alpha Zeta Society).

My first job out of college was with the American Stores Company in Pueblo, Colorado. During my two years there, my salary nearly doubled, but it was only a meat packing plant, and I really didn't enjoy the work. So, I decided to give sales a try, and got a second job representing Kirby vacuum cleaners. I'd begin my day at the packing plant at 5:00 a.m., go home after work, change clothes, and head out to sell Kirby's door-to-door, starting at 5:00 p.m. I also sold on weekends.

Selling turned out to be one of my greatest skills, and eventually, I took a job with Merck Pharmaceuticals in their animal health division. This position involved a move to Texas. After my first year, Merck recognized me as "Rookie of the Year," and I continued for four straight years as one of their top producers.

During my fourth year of employment, Merck hired a man by the name of Dick White. Dick had previously been with 3M Corporation in a sales training position, and he was one of the most fantastic guys I'd ever met. He really opened my eyes to the basic essentials of selling. He introduced me to the "FAB" concept: how to present the Features of a product, the Advantages of that product, and the Benefits of the product.

He told me that most salespeople stop after talking about the Features and Advantages, but never really get to the Benefits—and it's the Benefits that the customers really want. It's the Benefits that close the sale. The Benefits are the personal reasons why people buy. Dick believed that to close

## Background

a sale, a salesperson really needed to relate the purchase to a personal benefit of the product or service. As Zig Ziglar put it, "People don't buy for logical reasons. They buy for emotional reasons."

The concept of FAB was simple, true, and it made sense to me. I adopted that philosophy, and I've used it ever since. Candidly, FAB is one of the most amazing things I've learned in my life. It should be a part of every salesperson's Master Plan.

Dick taught me many other valuable lessons about sales. He said, "The sales department isn't the whole company, but the whole company had better be the sales department." I've tried to apply that lesson every day in every business I've been involved in. No matter what business you're in, even if you don't produce or sell any product, you're in the sales business. You're either selling a product or you're selling a service, so "the whole company had better be the sales department."

Because of applying the lessons I'd learned from Dick White, I was promoted several times and became responsible for conducting sales training meetings for distributors all over the county.

During my time with Merck, I came to realize that the sales reps were "representing" their products, not "selling them." In other words, they were "educating" the clientele—the veterinarians, the feedlot owners, and the people in the animal health industry—but they weren't "asking for an order." They were detail people, not salespeople. In contrast, I was actually *writing* orders, which I then turned over to the wholesale distributors—Merck's customers. They, of course, loved that! The more Merck products they sold, the more I helped them and the more we both prospered.

But a lot of the sales reps within the industry felt that asking for an order was beneath them and that doing so would make them common salespeople. There were lots of company reps out there, including those from Pfizer, Eli Lilly, and Upjohn. But I was one of the only reps writing a lot of orders every day and turning them in. I quickly earned a reputation within the industry.

The wholesale distributor salesmen realized they needed to get close to me because of the business I was writing. Merck only sold through distributors; consequently, those distributors learned very quickly that I was going to support them if they were writing business for Merck products and not for our competitors.

Because of my success at the very top of the sales charts, Merck tried to get me to move to the head office in New Jersey. In fact, they flew me there several times to interview for positions, but I had no interest in moving east. I've always loved the west too much to consider that.

In 1972, I left Merck to head up a new company, Tufts & Son of Oklahoma, Inc., which was loosely affiliated with Tufts & Son of Texas. The original company was founded by a wonderful friend and mentor, John Tufts, Sr. He was also in the animal health/pharmaceuticals industry and was interested in expanding his business into Oklahoma. John and I formed a partnership, and after putting up my farm as collateral, I became half owner of an exciting new venture.

We started small. I may have been the president, but I was also the only salesman. This suited me just fine because

Background

I love sales. I also had the good fortune to meet and hire Sheila, my first employee, who later became my wife. Why don't I let Sheila tell you about it?

When I was President at Tufts & Son of Oklahoma Inc. in the early 1970's.

With Betty Dalton and Sheila during a visit to Oklahoma City to plan the 35th reunion for Tufts & Son.

Tufts & Son warehouse in Oklahoma City, OK.

## Sheila

*It was 1972, and I was working at Stock Yards Bank in Oklahoma City. At first, I worked in the accounting department, but then they gave me a job as a kind of secretary, waiting on people at a desk right in the center of the lobby. I'd been working there about ten years at the time, and everyone in the bank was like family to me. Then one morning I arrived early, and as I tried to relock the door of the bank, a foot went inside the door. I couldn't lock it because a gentleman was standing on the other side, wanting to get in. I told him that the bank wasn't open yet, but he started to tell me everything he could to get inside. We went back and forth for a while, and then he said a bank officer with an unusual name told him he could use a desk and telephones upstairs because he was starting a new business. Trouble was, he couldn't remember the officer's name. We had an officer at the bank with an unusual name, and I was so gullible that I told it to him. "That's it! That's the guy's name," he said. And that's how Mike talked his way into the bank.*

*About a week later, Mike came back and told someone he was looking for the woman who had let him into the bank. He couldn't remember her name but thought it began with an "S." So they sent him over to me. He didn't recognize me at first because I used to wear wigs back then. The week before I'd been wearing this long brunette wig, but that day my wig was short and frosted. I looked like a totally different person. He said he wanted to talk to the person who does the hiring. He was opening up a veterinarian supply business in a warehouse just a block away. So, I put him in touch with the right person.*

*As he was leaving, he stopped to thank me, and I asked if I could come by his warehouse and pick up an application for*

## Background

*my sister who hated her job with the water department. He said he needed someone to manage the inside of the office, someone who could do accounting and sit at the front desk because he planned to be out selling as much as possible. After work, I swung by his warehouse to get an application for my sister. Mike looked at me and said, "I don't think your sister needs to come work for me. I think you need to come work for me."*

*I told him I wasn't looking for a job, that I was happy at the bank. He said, "I guess your job pays great." I told him it didn't, but I'd worked there for ten years and had lots of friends. Again, Mike said, "You need to come work for me." We went back and forth for a while, and then he said, "Let me take you to dinner and let's just talk about it. I have a list of things I can offer you that the bank will never be able to give you." I thought, "What can it hurt?" I went out to dinner, and he gave me the spiel. He offered double my salary, great insurance, and promised to send me on two or three trips every year. So, I gave the bank notice, and two weeks later, I was sitting at Mike's front desk in the warehouse. And everything Mike promised, he did.*

Tufts & Son started out with a small staff, but over time, we grew and eventually expanded into two other distribution companies—Western Vet and Sunwest Lawn and Garden—with a sales staff of a hundred and more than $100 million in annual sales.

With lots of hard work and by surrounding myself with good people, our success continued year after year. Until disaster struck. The energy companies in Texas and Oklahoma began to experience a severe economic crisis. Oil

## Background

came down from $40 a barrel to only about $8 a barrel. As a result, oil companies were not renewing their mineral leases with landowners and farmers. This created a tremendous cash flow problem for many of my customers, as well as for local banks.

In a matter of two years, over sixty banks in Oklahoma alone went out of business. The bank I did business with was taken over by the Federal Deposit Insurance Corporation (FDIC). With rising receivables past due, my loans were called. When I tried to secure financing from major banks on both coasts, I discovered that businesses in Oklahoma had been redlined, and no banks were loaning to companies in that state.

I also had another shock. During this turbulent time, I discovered that my "trusted" chief financial officer had actually been embezzling from the company to the tune of several hundred thousand dollars. It was a crushing blow on a personal level, as well as financial. One of my longtime friends, Dr. Jim Little, offered financing, but I didn't want to risk my friend's money. In the end, I sold out my companies and their divisions for pennies on the dollar.

The sale created much-needed cash, but it also created a tax issue in several of my subsidiary corporations. My accountant strongly recommended bankrupting those corporations, but I found the idea of bankruptcy unacceptable. Instead, I chose to use the sale proceeds to pay the tax bills.

One of my mentors taught me a very valuable lesson that I employ daily as part of my Master Plan: **FRIENDS COME AND GO, BUT ENEMIES ACCUMULATE.**

# Background

At this point in my life, it seemed I needed more friends.

Without a company and without money, I moved my family—my wife, Sheila, and our six children—from Oklahoma to Phoenix, Arizona, to start over.

There I was, beginning from square one again. I'll admit, those first few years were tough. It took me a while before I was able to buy my own house again. At that point, there was no way I could have ever dreamed about what was about to unfold in my life. The decision to move my family to the "Valley of the Sun" was driven by my belief that I would someday be successful in real estate. I never thought it possible I would own ranches in three different states, including two ranches that John Wayne had owned for more than forty years in Arizona—the Red River Ranch and the El Dorado Ranch.

Never did I dream I would own some of the top quarter horses in the nation.

Never in a million years did I envision being a partner in a major league baseball team, the Arizona Diamondbacks—a "newbie" team that won the World Series against the New York Yankees in 2001.

But the most significant successes in my life have nothing to do with ranches, sports, or business. They are, instead, very personal. Never did I imagine I would one day be the proud father of six children, the delighted grandfather of twenty-one grandchildren, and the joyful great-grandfather of twenty-one great grandchildren!

The opportunities and ultimate successes that came about as the result of the single decision to move to Arizona and start over have been astonishing . . . and the adventure continues! Although I highlight my involvement in this book, it's important to say that without my partners and team members working in concert with me, these accomplishments wouldn't have happened.

I hope the stories and lessons that I share in the following pages will engage you, inspire you, and empower you to create and follow your own Master Plan!

Sheila and me with just a portion of our ever-expanding family.

Kyle and Trina Roberts with Veronica and Dean Ingram enjoying an El Dorado Holdings Partners Cruise down the Nile.

# THE FIRST KEY: PEOPLE POWER

## CHAPTER ONE
# THE POWER OF RELATIONSHIPS

If you're like most people I've talked to, at some point in your life, a special person took you under his or her wing and became your mentor, your trusted advisor, your encourager, and your friend.

You may not have been looking for this person, you may not have expected this person to cross your path at the time and in the way it happened, and it may not have been until much later that you actually recognized the significant role they had in your life. Because I don't know what else to call these wonderful life surprises, I call them "Gifts from God."

My personal gift from God was a man named Virgil Haley, a successful farmer from New Mexico. I had known him practically from birth, but I didn't really appreciate him until I was thirteen years old.

**The Navajo Motel that my mom owned and managed after my dad's passing, and where I grew up.**

## 1. The Power of Relationships

I grew up in Roswell, New Mexico. You know, the small town where some alien spacecraft supposedly crash-landed. I don't know if that's truth or fiction because I never saw the crash site or any wreckage. And, I might add, I've never had contact with any extraterrestrial beings.

My childhood was average in every way imaginable. My parents owned and operated a small, thirty-four-unit motel known as "The Navajo." They worked hard to keep the place clean and inviting and to make every guest feel welcome. I learned a lot about the hospitality business by tagging along with my dad wherever he went.

**Yellowstone, 1954; Please don't feed the bears!**

My parents were very religious. We were regulars at the nearby Christian church and both of them were involved with church programs. It's not surprising that my faith has been an important part of my life. I learned the importance of God in my life at an early age.

**Mom and Dad in their early married years.**

When I was thirteen, the unimaginable happened and my *average* changed forever. My father died that year. He'd been battling cancer for three years. My dad was my best friend who did everything with me, and his death was a tremendous loss. Unfortunately, he had no health insurance, leaving my mom with a young son, an aging motel with a big mortgage, and a huge stack of medical and hospital bills. I'd always helped out at the motel, but overnight, I became the man of the house and assistant keeper of the inn. With the bills piling up and the mortgage looming, there was no longer the luxury of having a large staff to help with the motel chores. Instead, there was just a frightened widow and a thirteen-year-old kid.

**I guess I always knew what I really wanted to be!**

**Mom, Dad and me in front of the Navajo Motel.**

## 1. The Power of Relationships

I spent the rest of my school years getting up very early, cleaning rooms before school, and working at the motel afterward. I became the chambermaid, desk clerk, porter, switchboard operator, maintenance man (which included cleaning the never-ending parade of clogged toilets in the middle of the night), pool man, and snow removal expert. I learned at a very early age that if a job has to be done, complaining about it doesn't make it happen. I learned a bit about marketing too. After sunset, I'd go around the property, turning on the porch lights at every unit. I wanted to make sure, if someone happened to come by, the motel wouldn't appear dark and unwelcoming.

Every month, as the mortgage payment came due, I worried my mom wasn't going to be able to rent enough rooms to make it. Summers were easier, as tourist traffic rolled through town. But winter months were very quiet.

**Ray Farley, Virgil Haley, my lifetime mentor and E.J. Bennett.**

During the summers, I could also help out a little more with the finances. A local farmer, Virgil Haley, would pick me up late at night, and I would bale hay for him until

## 1. The Power of Relationships

sunup. He paid me a dollar an hour—fairly good money back then! After working the fields, I'd catch a couple hours of sleep, then head off to my other job as a lifeguard at the local public swimming pool. I'd get back to the motel at 1:00 p.m. for a little rest, before tourists started arriving around 4:00 or 5:00 p.m.

Throughout those years, it was Virgil who became my personal Gift from God. He was my friend, my encourager, and my employer—and in many respects, a second father to me. Virgil had six sons of his own, so many people in Roswell assumed I was his seventh son. That idea was reinforced when I'd go to the store to pick up something for him and then sign for it with "Haley Farms" (with his permission, of course).

Not only was Virgil able to keep me gainfully employed, but he also took me hunting and fishing. As the youth leaders at my church, he and his wife gave me hope and inspired me during difficult times. They instilled a lot of values in my life, values that are still at the core of my life principles today. Virgil was always there for the teenagers, especially for *this* teenager. He never stopped giving . . . and I will forever be grateful to him.

I continued to work at the motel, as a lifeguard, and on Virgil's farm until I went away to college in 1962. Thankfully, my mother was able to pay off the mortgage on the Navajo in 1964. She sold it and retired in 1979.

Take a moment and think back on your own life, about people you knew who were generous toward you and what an impact they had on your life. It's never too late to thank them. I still tell Virgil, who is now ninety-eight and still

## 1. The Power of Relationships

drives a tractor, how much he means to me every time I have the opportunity.

But as important as Virgil is to me to this day, my mother, Maude Ingram, was a thousand times more important. I did my best to tell her how much I loved her and how she had impacted my life in endless, wonderful ways . . . until that sad day in 2009 when she left our world. Now I wish I had told her every day.

**When in Egypt . . .**

Above all others, there is a very special person to whom I say, "I love you" every day. That's my wife, Sheila. She's wonderful! She always looks for the good in people; in every situation she creates the model all of us should follow.

I am a believer in the institution of marriage, or better yet, the joys of marriage. If you're not closer to your spouse than any other person, you're missing out on the best. Sheila and I aren't just husband and wife bound by a piece of paper. We're friends, mutual confidantes, involved parents, co-workers, and above all, spiritual partners. We travel together, socialize with friends together, laugh together, learn together, worship together, and pray together. Sheila blesses every day of my life!

Through my mother, Sheila, Virgil, and many others who came into my life, I have discovered the reasons why meaningful relationships are so important . . . and what it takes to make them work.

## The Value of Meaningful Relationships

First, a healthy, meaningful relationship is open and honest. In this book, I discuss my thoughts on such topics as trust, integrity, and forgiveness. I see these as just some of the elements of an open and honest relationship.

Second, meaningful relationships are mutually supportive—truly a two-way street. This works in my marriage because Sheila and I have shared values, so I know she will support me and she knows I will support her.

Third, relationships are the key to building the career you desire. One of the best examples I know of success through relationships is that of my friend, Red Steagall. If you haven't heard of him, you're missing out on a great treat.

## Red Steagall

Red got his start riding bulls in rodeos. He planned to go to college on a football scholarship and become a

## 1. The Power of Relationships

large-animal vet, but he developed polio and lost strength in his left shoulder and arm. There was no longer a scholarship, but Red worked day and night to get himself through college. Meanwhile, Red was rebuilding strength in the fingers of his left hand by teaching himself to play the guitar. He even had a band in college. After Red got his degree in agriculture, he worked for the next five years in agricultural chemistry.

Then he gave it all up for a career in music. A couple of his friends moved to Hollywood to produce music, and Red packed his bags and joined them. He wrote a song called "Here We Go Again," and convinced Ray Charles to record it. The song was a hit. Since then, it's been re-recorded sixty-three times by artists such as Nancy Sinatra, Johnny Duncan, and Roy Clark. Red is spending the rest of his life composing, performing, and promoting country music.

Other country music performers may have had more hits than Red, but I don't believe any have had a greater impact on country music. He's recorded twenty-six consecutive records that tracked on the national charts and has released a total of twenty-two albums. Over 200 of his compositions were recorded by him and other artists. Red received the Wrangler Award for Original Music five times and has composed, co-written, or performed with a number of country music legends, including George Strait, Hank Snow, Nancy Sinatra, Glen Campbell, Toby Keith, Charley Pride, Charlie Daniels, and many others.

This guy's got friends everywhere—everywhere in rural America and everywhere in rodeo circles. I don't know anybody with so many "best friends." It's how he

## 1. The Power of Relationships

makes people feel. He greets everyone as if they're the most important person in his life. Plus, he's made a difference in a lot of people's lives. I know Reba McEntire will never forget him. He discovered Reba back in 1974 when she sang the national anthem at the National Rodeo Finals in Oklahoma City. He was so impressed with her voice that he helped get her signed with Mercury Records. We all know what a great career she's had since then. In 2024, when Reba sang the national anthem again, this time at the Super Bowl, she pointed out to Red that it was fifty years since he'd discovered her singing it for the first time. What a memory!

One of Red's greatest goals is to preserve Western history and its culture. He teaches other people about the history of the West, its traditions, and its values. He and I grew up in an agrarian society where people were forced to depend on each other. For that to happen, people needed to live by a value system that includes honesty, loyalty, and respect. They still do. Red believes that those values can be found in what he calls the "Good Book" or the Bible.

Since 1991, Red has hosted the "Red Steagall Cowboy Gathering" in Fort Worth. It's an authentic Western experience, featuring a rodeo, a nightly country swing festival and dance, as well as country music and poetry. Fans come from all over the nation to attend. Besides making appearances on syndicated television shows, Red had his own radio and television shows, including "Red Steagall Is Somewhere West of Wall Street," which features stories about the history of the West. He also hosts "Cowboy Corner," which is broadcast weekly on 170 radio stations in forty-three states.

## 1. The Power of Relationships

Not only was Red inducted into the Texas Cowboy Hall of Fame and the National Cowboy & Western Heritage Museum, but he was also named the Official Cowboy Poet of Texas. A life-size statue of Red riding his horse now sits on the east lawn of the Cowtown Coliseum in Fort Worth. Bruce Greene, a renowned Western artist, created the statue to honor the man who has contributed so much to our Western heritage.

**Red presenting me with "The Code of the West".**

Over the past fifty years, Red has impacted and influenced me more than anyone can imagine. I have reprinted many of his poems and songs, but the best book about Red is his new book, *Texas Red*, which he recently published. I strongly recommend everyone read this book.

1. The Power of Relationships

I am a proud "Red's Ranger." About 20 years ago, Red started conducting a History Tour every summer with thirty-five of his best friends. We called ourselves "Red's Bus Cowboys." Later, we adopted the name Red's Rangers. We have traveled the nation and parts of Canada studying the American West, its formative years, and some of its wars. As we traveled, all dressed in pressed, starched jeans and shirts and cowboy hats, we got a lot of attention. Everywhere we went, people would stop us and ask, "Who are you guys?" One year someone said, "We're retired Texas Rangers." Don't let the truth get in the way of a good story. I would say each one of us would claim Red to be his best friend.

Me, Marc Myers, Red Steagall, Mike Rose, Gary Kinslow and Trent Willmon – on a great trip riding strong with Red's Rangers.

We are all very excited to be involved in the planning stage of the Red Steagall Institute for Traditional Western Arts to be built at the National Ranching Heritage Center, a thirty-plus acre institute and historical park on the campus of Texas Tech University in Lubbock. This center is envisioned to create an environment where current Western craftsmen in traditional skills such as saddle making, boot making, metal working, poetry, song writing, painting, and sculpture will work hand in hand with artists of the future to preserve these Western art forms for years to come.

Red's collection of his Western artifacts, including his song and poetry manuscripts and copies of his television and radio shows, will be showcased at the Institute. I was so proud when Red invited my very close friend and the longest living partner I have in El Dorado Holdings, Larry Williams, to become a Red's Ranger. Larry, after building a very successful lumber business, sold that company and became one of the nation's largest cattlemen with 10,000 mother cows on ranches scattered from Idaho to Oregon and Nevada to Montana.

Larry is the ultimate friend to me, Red Steagall, and now all the other Rangers. He rides for the brand. "Ride for the Brand" is Red's motto and ours. Red says that he built his career on the foundation of his diverse relationships. One of those relationships, I'm happy to say, is with me. We talk on the phone almost every day of the week. Denise, my assistant, says it's more like several times a day. As Red says, "We have a lot to talk about." Red Steagall isn't only a friend, he's also a partner in El Dorado investment properties.

1. The Power of Relationships

Me with two of my very best friends and partners, Red Steagall and Larry Williams, enjoying long friendships in God's nature.

## Johnny Trotter

Red introduced me to Johnny Trotter, another person who understands the value of relationships. You may be surprised to hear that Johnny does many of his deals with a simple handshake. He's honest, trustworthy, follows through on his commitments, and expects his business partners will do the same. Johnny's commitment to relationships makes people want to seek him out and be a part of whatever he does.

1. The Power of Relationships

Johnny is president of one of the largest cattle feeding operations in the nation and owns a large Ford dealership in Hereford, Texas. He sits on the boards of several banks and owns ranches in several states. Even though Johnny is busy with his numerous business enterprises, he's given his valuable time and experience to the American Quarter Horse Association, where he's served as president on the Executive Commission. As a lifetime member myself, I value his commitment.

**Me and Johny Trotter, one of the best friends and partners a guy could have, at the "Cowboy"—the National Cowboy and Western Heritage Museum in Oklahoma City.**

Red Steagall and I were honored to introduce Johnny when he was presented with the Chester A. Reynolds Memorial Award from the National Cowboy & Western

## 1. The Power of Relationships

Heritage Museum. The award is given to an individual for unwavering commitment to the future of the American West. No one is more deserving of this award than Johnny.

I began my introduction by saying, "Anyone could have found success if they had the inheritance that he received." You may think it means he came into a lot of money, but no, it was something much *better.* He was born the son of a Methodist preacher who was a pastor with Johnny's mother. You could find Johnny in the front row at that small Texas town church each and every Sunday.

Johnny's inheritance was much greater than money. He learned the Ten Commandments, the Golden Rule, and to love others as yourself. He also learned it was better to give than to receive. It was the right foundation for success. Johnny's word is his bond. His name stands for integrity. That night, his mother was sitting at the front table, beaming from pride and with tears in her eyes.

Johnny is owner of Ruidoso Downs Race Track, home to the nation's richest Quarter Horse race held each year in New Mexico. After he purchased it, he had a new chapel constructed at the track for the use of the owners, trainers, jockeys, and visitors.

I was happy to welcome him into his first investment with El Dorado several years ago, and he has been a part of every investment since then. I hope to partner with him for years to come.

### Jimmy Walker

A couple years ago, there was an article about Jimmy Walker in *Newsweek* entitled "The Man Who Schmoozed the

World." I couldn't agree more. In fact, Jimmy wrote a book on the same subject called *It's All About Relationships*.

Jimmy Walker is an insurance agent, just a regular guy with an unusual list of clients, including well-known businesspeople, super-star athletes, and famous stars in the entertainment industry. How does that make him special enough to get an article in *Newsweek*? The most important thing you need to know is that Jimmy has a heart of gold, and I'm not the only one who says so. Just ask Mark Cuban, Reba McEntire, Billy Crystal, Michael Jordan, and Lonnie Ali, wife of the late Muhammad Ali.

Jimmy is a people person who believes in helping others. Back in 1994, he started an annual fundraising event for charity called "Celebrity Fight Night." It started off by placing athletes, like Charles Barkley, in a mock boxing arena. But Jimmy didn't feel it was successful enough. So, two years later, he changed the format from fighting to entertainment. He talked Muhammad Ali into being spokesperson for the event, which would raise money for Parkinson's disease. Jimmy also brought on legendary music producer David Foster, whom he met at the 1996 Grammy Awards. Then he asked Reba McEntire to emcee, which she did for fifteen years. In all that time, Celebrity Fight Night has raised approximately $90 million for charities. Today Jimmy is the Chairman of Celebrity Adventures, raising money for the Andrea Bocelli Foundation, Grace Sober Living, and Barrow Neurological Institute.

How does he do it? Jimmy has no shame when it comes to asking people he doesn't know to help him raise money for charity. Everyone who participates does so as a volunteer.

## 1. The Power of Relationships

That's why the *Newsweek* article about Jimmy was titled "The Man Who Schmoozed the World." In other words, you better watch out if Jimmy is headed your way!

Jimmy's philanthropy started way before Celebrity Fight Night. In 1982, he founded a program in his backyard— "Bicycles for Kids." The program has grown into an annual event in downtown Phoenix, benefiting inner-city children who can't afford a bike. In addition to the bike giveaways, they also provide food baskets for the families. Since its inception, the program has given away over 8,000 bicycles to children in need.

In 2007, Jimmy initiated another program— "Never Give Up." Every Monday, he visits 500 to 600 homeless people at St. Vincent DePaul for breakfast. Jimmy usually brings a business leader or professional athlete with him to provide inspirational words to those in need.

Keep making friends, Jimmy! You make the world a better place!

### Boysie Bollinger

Now I'd like you to meet my friend Donald T. "Boysie" Bollinger. Boysie's father owned a machine shop in a Louisiana shipyard and built a family house right in the middle of it. Boysie literally grew up in his dad's company. When Boysie finished college, he went to work at the shipyard. No coat and tie; his business suit was boots and jeans. In 1984, when oil went from $40 a barrel to $8 a barrel, their business suffered, so Boysie obtained a government contract to build patrol boats for the Coast Guard. Since 1984, the company has built every Coast Guard patrol

## 1. The Power of Relationships

boat—approximately 160 boats. Over time, Boysie's business expanded to fourteen shipyards, becoming the largest government/commercial shipyard in America.

Boysie says, "In the early years, all my customers were friends. We did things together as friends and as business relationships. I'm a strong believer in relationships. I don't need to be in business with people who are not honest, and I surely don't want to be in business with people I don't know and don't agree with. As people, we should never forget that relationships are important."

When Boysie first checked out El Dorado's real estate investment opportunities, he told me, "I wanted to see who you were more than I wanted to see what the real estate was. And the more I saw the people around you and how you operate, the more I was glad to be investing with you. It's not about money; it's about building something together." I couldn't agree more. Once again, it's important to remember **FRIENDS COME AND GO, BUT ENEMIES ACCUMULATE**. Don't get more enemies than you can afford.

Boysie was a driving force and a leading contributor in the conception and development of the National World War II Museum, founded in 2000 and located in New Orleans. He currently sits on the board of trustees. The museum was designated by the U.S. Congress as America's official National World War II Museum in 2004. It highlights America's experience in World War II and the sacrifices made to ensure our freedoms.

The bottom line in all this is simple. I discovered it from my mother and from Virgil and others in the intervening years—and especially from Sheila. There is power and beauty in relationships. Value them. Nurture them. And give back in every way you can. They are a vital part of your Master Plan.

## CHAPTER TWO
## THE POWER OF NETWORKING

There's an old axiom that seems to apply to both life and business: "It's not *what* you know, it's *who* you know," and I don't mean that in a negative way.

While I definitely believe in acquiring knowledge and wisdom, it's not so much *what I've learned* that has built my ventures. It's the *people* who have come into my life. This, of course, connects back to the value of relationships. Another axiom is, "People don't care how much you know until they know how much you care."

I believe in opening my mind and heart to all sorts of relationships. Over the years, people have told me that my ability to find common ground with them is my most intriguing quality. It's enabled me to accomplish some very difficult endeavors in my life, from getting a road built and designated as a state highway to obtaining zoning changes everyone said couldn't be done. I've found that if I can get a group of people to focus on their commonalities rather than their differences, I can accomplish all sorts of things. Amazing things!

I can tell you that I've built long-lasting relationships with people of many nationalities, faiths, and ethnic origins. Because I live and work in Arizona, some of my best friends are Native American. I cherish these friendships and those I have with people from many other backgrounds.

## 2. The Power of Networking

I've also worked hard to develop relationships with people who have different political views. I have great friends who are Democrats, Republicans, and Independents. True, there are times you may not get individuals with different beliefs to agree; however, you may find that you're closer to agreement than you originally believed if you can build a relationship.

**With Tom Brokaw, we are on opposite sides of many current issues, but I still consider him to be a true American Patriot and great friend.**

Among my good friends who express different political views from mine are Tom Brokaw and Brian Greenspun. Tom, of course, is one of the world's best-known news anchors. He's the only person to have hosted all of the major NBC news shows, including "The Today Show," "NBC Nightly News," and "Meet the Press." He's also the author of the wonderful book, *The Greatest Generation*.

Brian is the developer of the very successful Green Valley master-planned development in Henderson, Nevada.

He's also the president and publisher of *The Las Vegas Sun* newspaper.

**With Brian Greenspun, President and Publisher of *The Las Vegas Sun* newspaper, we are good friends who are also often on different sides politically.**

I enjoy any time I'm able to spend with these two good men; however, when we're together, we concentrate on things we have in common rather than areas of disagreement. I've known both these gentlemen for a number of years and we've simply agreed to disagree. We may discuss our opinions but always leave as friends. I can't believe I haven't been able to convince them of my views, and I'm sure they feel the same way.

The significance of building relationships is something I discovered very early in my life. It's the first step in unleashing the power of networking. I believe there are four ways in which we network:

1. Other people come to us with their vision, ideas, connections, and opportunities.
2. We go to other people with our visions, ideas, connections, and opportunities.
3. Other people or situations connect us, maybe as the result of recommendations from satisfied clients or through various types of "lead groups."
4. God "does His thing." (If you don't believe in God, you can call this fate, or chance, or the law of the universe.) I've experienced too many things in my life that I couldn't explain—apart from God. You can accept or reject this as you choose, of course.

## Harvey Mackay

Let me tell you about my friend Harvey Mackay. Early in life, Harvey had many jobs, including selling magazines door-to-door, delivering newspapers, removing snow (with a shovel), and mowing lawns. When Harvey graduated college, he became an envelope salesman for Quality Park Envelope Company. He also joined Minneapolis's Oak Ridge Country Club. It was to play golf, he told them, but it was really to network with the area businessmen. With his networking, Harvey became Quality Park's top salesman. Five years later, he used his proceeds to purchase an insolvent envelope company that he grew into a multi-million-dollar business. In 2000, he sold that company, while remaining an equal partner and chairman.

Harvey went on to become a successful writer and

international speaker. His first book, *Swim with the Sharks Without Being Eaten Alive*, was on the *New York Times* bestseller list for fifty-four weeks and sold more than five million copies. He followed it with other bestsellers, including *ABCs of Business Success*, *Getting a Job Is a Job*, and *Beware the Naked Man Who Offers You His Shirt*. His inspirational business books have sold more than ten million copies in eighty countries and been translated into forty-six languages. Besides his exceptional writing career, he is a highly sought-after speaker, including at Fortune 1000 companies around the world. Harvey is the type of person who brightens up any room he enters and one of the best networkers I've had the pleasure to know.

## Bill Burch

You might like to hear how networking helped me in my own business. For a moment, let me take you back into my history. You may recall how I resigned from Merck in 1972 and left Colorado in my rear-view mirror. I relocated to Oklahoma City, where I built a successful career and three separate businesses selling veterinary medicines to farmers, ranchers, farm stores, and veterinarians.

In 1974, this expanded to include a new subsidiary, Sunwest Lawn and Garden. Homer Lacky, a former Pfizer representative, took the lead and built Sunwest into one of the largest distribution companies in that field. We became the leading supplier to garden centers in five Southwest states. This included privately owned garden centers and also centers located within Kmart, Target, Home Depot, and

## 2. The Power of Networking

other major retail chains. This company was sold in 1983 to Garden America, a division of Weyerhaeuser.

Jim Graber, the leading salesperson at Diamond Labs, and Jim Keller, the president at Abbot Labs, both joined in our venture. In 1978, we formed another subsidiary known as Western Veterinarian Supply, which sold products exclusively to veterinarians. In 1984, I sold both Western Vet and Tufts & Son of Oklahoma to Walco International.

As I mentioned earlier, things turned from great to awful during the oil crisis of the 1980s. No banks would make loans to companies in Oklahoma or Texas—no matter what the industry—and I had to sell the business and all my assets. I am a salesman, and I sold everything! To keep my family going, I considered a job in Dallas, but Sheila didn't want to move to Texas. Her roots were in Oklahoma City, where her entire family lived. Plus, she thought it would be hard on the kids if we uprooted them.

Then, along came an interesting suggestion from a master networker named Bill Burch. Bill insisted that I not sign a contract to move to Dallas. Instead, he invited me to visit him in Arizona. I traveled with Bill down to Tucson for a meeting and had the opportunity to meet wonderful businesspeople from both Phoenix and Tucson. Since I was a history buff, I was excited to see Picacho Peak, where the Western-most battle of the Civil War took place.

That night, Bill and I were sitting in his backyard hot tub, looking up through the palm trees at the moon. I said, "This is about as close to heaven as I think I could be." I remember it clearly. It was the ninth of February and a perfect winter night in Arizona.

## 2. The Power of Networking

**My lifelong friend, Dr. Bill Burch (I call him "Willy") who brought me to Arizona.**

When I got out of the hot tub, I called home to check in with Sheila. I asked her, "How's everything in Oklahoma City?"

She replied, "Well, we didn't have school today. There was a huge ice storm, so school was cancelled."

Hmm . . . not a good day, I thought. I realized it was the perfect time to introduce a new concept, so I said, "Sheila, we're moving to Arizona."

Boy, was I wrong! Sheila burst into tears. She'd already done her level best to accept the fact that we were moving to Dallas, which was three hours' drive time and one-hour flight time away from three of our six kids who were already enrolled in college! *And* her three sisters! *And* her mom and

## 2. The Power of Networking

dad, whom she'd never been away from in her entire life! Now I'd upset the apple cart *again*?

I said with as much enthusiasm as I could muster, "Sheila, you're going to love Arizona."

She wasn't sure about that at all! *And* she told me so.

Two weeks later, I brought the whole family out to Arizona during spring break. Sheila cried throughout the entire trip. Her eyes were almost swollen shut by the time we hit Phoenix.

I thought I had a great sales strategy, bringing them down to Phoenix through Sedona and its red rocks—the stunning beauty of Arizona. Now I wasn't so sure.

But when we arrived in Phoenix and our kids saw the palm trees and the green grass, the tide turned. You have to realize this was March, and there wasn't a lot of green grass in Oklahoma. They said, "Oh wow, Dad, this is really cool!"

Sheila looked around and said, "Shut up, kids."

She was not impressed with Arizona at all. She still didn't want to leave Oklahoma, but I felt in my bones that it was the right business decision, the one that would allow me to provide for my family. I went ahead and moved out to Arizona alone the next month. I wanted to begin fresh and operate my own business again. The idea of working for someone else in Dallas, after having owned my own company, didn't appeal to me.

A few weeks later, Sheila and my mother-in-law reluctantly loaded a U-Haul truck and drove it to Arizona.

Thanks to Bill Burch's networking efforts, we got off to a fast start in our new city. Bill immediately introduced me to people I never imagined I'd know. In 1987, I co-founded the company that still exists today—El Dorado Holdings, Inc.

## 2. The Power of Networking

The mission of our company was (and still is) to buy land, which some said was worthless, and transform it into something significant. To accomplish this, we needed to find investors who could capture our vision and believe in the future. I had no money—for reasons I introduced earlier—so I needed what I call OPM (Other People's Money).

Naturally, some of our first investors were people Bill Burch introduced to us in Arizona, as well as friends and business associates in Oklahoma. Bill personally invested $8,500 of his hard-earned money with us in 1992. Because he placed his trust in my idea that money could be made on "worthless" land, I had to prove to him and my other investors that I could help them get what they wanted—a return on their investment.

My good friend, the late Zig Ziglar, often said, "You will get all you want in life if you help enough other people get what they want." I've demonstrated that those words are true.

This is what networking is all about. If you help people get what they want, you become a part of their networks, and they'll bring you more new relationships and more business than you could possibly imagine. In almost forty years in business, we've never advertised for an investor or gone out publicly looking for one.

You can build a business on networking, and it can become loyal, repeat business. Many of the people to whom Bill Burch introduced me 20 or 35 years ago are still investors. Some have participated in every investment I've offered. Now their children and grandchildren are continuing with us.

I'm proud to say my investors have been paid well for their trust. One of them recently told me, "I've never done as well on any of my other investments." In fact, Bill Burch himself paid a visit to our office in late 2017. He asked us, "How much money have I made with my investments in El Dorado Holdings?" We did the calculations and replied, "Your initial investment of $8,500 and your reinvestments have generated over $1.6 million in distributions (that's about $900 thousand in profits), and your remaining property assets are valued at over $900 thousand." He was elated and wanted to know when the next investment opportunity would be available.

## Networking is a Two-Way Street

The Bible talks about planting seeds and harvesting "a hundred-fold." These words actually apply today when the seeds fall on good soil. Networking prepares your company for fruitful business relationships, just as tilling and fertilizer prepare good soil for a future harvest.

At this point, you might be thinking, "Mike just uses his networks to make more money." Believe it or not, my life is not all about money. But money can accomplish a lot of good, when used in the right ways. I seek to do exactly that.

Today, my personal goal is not simply to build a business through networking, but to help create value in other people's lives. I want to help them with their passions and support their charities of choice. Yes, their charities need to be compatible with my personal beliefs, but I'm not narrow-minded about it. If people are truly helped—and the charities are not pointlessly enriched—I can usually get behind them.

## 2. The Power of Networking

Ultimately, I believe that networking should be a two-way street and not only to your advantage. Many times, my sole benefit from networking is to help another person. I believe that if you help someone, they'll be much more likely to help someone else. The people who've helped me in my life have certainly empowered me to help others. But if you see the power of networking as something that works only on your behalf, you won't enjoy the benefits that come from the giving side of the equation. I learned this from Bill Burch, and I continue to apply what I have learned from Zig Ziglar. It's a lesson that's proven more valuable to me than any I learned in school.

Bob Buford wrote a great book called *Half Time*, and his ministry was all about half time in life, simply going from success to a life of significance, a life that will continue long after we have departed this world. You spend the first half of your life raising a family and building accomplishments. Use the second half to influence others.

I encourage you to learn more about charities such as Childhelp. Childhelp was started around sixty-five years ago by two movie stars, Sara O'Meara and Yvonne Fedderson. Today, they have created the largest child advocacy organization in the world with a hotline for abused children in every state in the union.

Sheila and I are very involved in Christian education. We love what Dr. Larry Arnn is doing as president of Hillsdale College, located in Hillsdale, Michigan. The college is a strong supporter of the U.S. Constitution and the values this country was founded on, especially the Bill of Rights.

Just remember this: People are important. To get what *you* want out of life, help them get what *they* want. It all

## 2. The Power of Networking

starts with relationships, relationships that you build on by networking.

Sarah Palin—former Governor of Alaska and 2008 Vice Presidential candidate—a good friend and partner, spending time at the ranch.

Me with some great El Dorado Holdings partners and friends—Craig and Hazel Dance, Boysie Bollinger, Wes Bates, John Thodos, and Robert Sparks at a political event.

## CHAPTER THREE
# THE POWER OF PARTNERSHIPS

*"As iron sharpens iron, so one person sharpens another."*

Those words are from Proverbs 27:17 (NIV Bible). To me, it's an indication that the one-on-one concept is the way things should work. Life is better when you have partners with whom you can share ideas, enjoy events, and build businesses.

Yet, many people in today's world are skeptical of partnerships. That's because they've seen businesses fail and partners go at each other's throats. They've also watched as marriages have failed and torn families apart.

I believe there's a way to build a partnership that will last. I call it the "Common Good."

In partnerships that work:

1. There's a shared goal—the pursuit of a shared outcome.
2. Everyone is an equal. Even if investments aren't the same, the payoff is based fairly on the investor's proportionate share.
3. When one wins, all win.
4. One success leads to future successes.
5. When one loses, all lose (sad, but true).
6. If there's a loss, you both learn from it and move forward.

## 3. The Power of Partnerships

Dan Adams, Wes Bates and Richard Childress at Richard Childress Racing (RCR).

## Richard Childress

I recently had an interesting conversation with a good friend, Richard Childress. You may know his name because he's been involved in NASCAR for years. He founded Richard Childress Racing (RCR) in 1969 and currently has three or four racing teams on the circuit. Richard has more than 200 victories across NASCAR'S top three series and seventeen championships. He's the first in NASCAR'S history to win championships in all three national touring series. His team has racked up three Daytona 500 wins, as well as three Brickyard 400 victories. Richard is one of the top three names in racing today. In 2017, he was inducted into the NASCAR Hall of Fame.

How has Richard Childress managed to accomplish all

## 3. The Power of Partnerships

this? By assembling a team of dedicated partners. Some team members have been with him for over thirty years. They have one shared goal—winning races. He finds investors and sponsors who have a vested interest in that outcome. They all know they'll be faced with both wins and losses. But losses never deter them from pursuing the win. They simply learn from those losses and move on. When Richard retired from active driving in 1981, the #3 car was driven by Ricky Rudd and then Dale Ernhardt in 1984. In 1998 Earnhardt won Daytona driving the #3 car. In the early 2000s Austin and Ty (Richard's grandsons) began racing. In 2018, Austin won the most coveted race, the Daytona 500, in overtime. Richard's other grandson, Ty, is now also part of the RCR team.

Of course, Richard's most successful and strongest partnership is with his wife, Judy. Engraved on a plaque on her desk are the following words: **"Whatever women do they must do twice as well as men to be thought half as good. Luckily, this is not difficult."**

Those are the words of Charlotte Whitton, the first female mayor of a major city in Canada (Ottawa) back in 1951. Whitton was clearly no shrinking violet, and neither is Judy. I have found these ladies' words to be profound. I'll talk about the Power of Women later.

Richard's principles for building successful partnerships are simple:

- Have a clear dream.
- Find and empower great people.
- Become unified in the pursuit of that dream.

And that's the power of partnerships!

## 3. The Power of Partnerships

### Investor Partnerships at El Dorado Holdings

You may wonder how partnerships work at our company, El Dorado Holdings. Before El Dorado existed, I occasionally invested in other people's business opportunities, but they were limited partnerships. In limited partnerships, the general partner has all the power and the limited partners have none. Usually, these partnerships were structured with substantial upfront and ongoing fees to the general partner. It only took a couple of these ventures to determine that they were not for me.

When I started El Dorado, I wanted my investors to be partners with me. I didn't just want their money. I sought their input and wanted them to feel they were a part of the deal, not sitting on the outskirts waiting for something to happen. I began to structure El Dorado's investments as general partnerships, which I converted to limited liability companies when that structure became available in Arizona. Every time we create a new opportunity for an investment in land or buildings, we set up a Limited Liability Company—an LLC. Because of problems I had in the past, I remain averse to bank lending, except for some income-producing properties. Otherwise, I prefer to raise cash for all other investment opportunities.

In Arizona and many other states, LLCs can be set up in one of two ways. They can either be "manager-managed" or they can be "member-managed." In El Dorado's LLCs, all my investors and I are members. Our LLCs are member-managed, and El Dorado is only the day-to-day manager. In other words, El Dorado is subject to the members' will. That means the other members—the investors—can get together at any time and decide by majority vote to fire me.

It also means that the members decide when and at what price to sell, or even not to sell. All major decisions are made as a group, and our team works diligently to make sure that all members are kept informed of all activities, including local, regional, and even national news that could affect their particular investment.

Even though I'm the one who initially established the LLC, I have to perform. I have to do my job. People often ask me, "Mike, how do you protect yourself?" The answer is always the same: I make sure the members are pleased with my performance. If you are doing a good job, you won't be replaced.

In successful partnerships, the people with the responsibility to perform do exactly that. To date, El Dorado has formed over 130 LLCs that include over 83,000 acres of land. We've entitled and/or developed close to 50,000 residential lots, several thousand acres of commercial/retail property, and several golf courses. In addition, we've owned and managed approximately 250,000 square feet of office space and over 1,300 apartment units. All of these ventures are LLCs controlled by our investors—our partners.

## My Employees Are My Partners Too

In the same sense, employees can and should become partners in your business. In fact, I don't even like the word "employee." I prefer "team member." In an ideal situation, the employer and the team member become partners in the

## 3. The Power of Partnerships

sense that they have shared goals and shared responsibilities for a successful outcome.

**The best staff a man could ask for!**

Of all the people I've been fortunate enough to work with over the years, my most valued right-hand assistant has been Denise Organ. She's not only a loyal team member, but she's also family to Sheila and me. Her husband, Scott, and her kids are all family too. I've had many executive assistants during the over forty-eight years I've been in business, but I can honestly say that no one comes close to Denise. She has an uncanny ability to know what needs to be done before I do and is always one step ahead. I know my busy schedule and travel would be a challenge to almost anyone, but Denise handles it with professionalism and tact. Her judgment and diplomacy during difficult situations are unparalleled. I would truly be lost without her, so I try to make sure she's happy in her position and never leaves.

## 3. The Power of Partnerships

As I walk around our office and see the people who work here today, I feel that each and every one of them is a family member. I told them when they came to work at El Dorado that they should tear up their resumes because they'll never need to look for another job. Even in downturns—in a terrible real estate recession like the one we went through in recent years—we've not had to lay off one team member. I'm thankful for that. We really need one another to build our future together.

### My Partnerships Go Way Back

My experience with successful partnerships goes back to my association with John Tufts, years ago, when I lived in Oklahoma City. Although I'd had a successful career with Merck Pharmaceuticals, when John Tufts, Sr. entered my life and offered me a partnership in Tufts & Son of Oklahoma, my world changed in ways I never dreamed. My task was to open up new distributorship locations that represented more than 300 companies, primarily in Oklahoma, to start.

In 1980, I brought in my best friend in life, Roy McKay, president of McKay Oil Company, as an investor, so that we could expand into additional states. Eventually, that company and its subsidiaries expanded into five other states.

In 1985, I moved to Arizona and eventually founded El Dorado Holdings, Inc. with Monty Ortman. We'd both moved to Arizona at about the same time and were introduced by a mutual friend. Both of us were starting over in our lives, so it was a good match. For twenty-three years, we had one of the greatest partnerships I've ever seen.

## 3. The Power of Partnerships

When Monty called one day and said he wanted to spend more time with his kids and grandkids, I agreed to buy his share of our partnership. The partnership may have been over, but our friendship continued.

These partnerships are successful because the partners all seek the "Common Good." Other people may build their businesses through relationships with big corporations and big investment funds. But how can those arrangements result in real relationships?

I've chosen to build my business through partnerships with other entrepreneurial businesspeople. These partnerships turn into genuine relationships. We fish together, we hunt together, and we travel together. In a very real sense, I am a part of their family and they're a part of my family. I have investors today who have a key to my home in Phoenix and know they're welcome to "check themselves in" to our guest house. They feel comfortable enough to stay at our house, whether we're home or not. It's been that way for over thirty years. My investors are my partners and my family.

You should have no doubt that there is power in partnerships. To make them work, you have to invest your time and keep the idea of the "Common Good" in mind always. Good things in life rarely happen by accident. Successful partnerships are the result of attention and intention.

3. The Power of Partnerships

My Texas partner, John Tufts (right) with his dad, WG Tufts.

No genie required—Skip Rimsza, partner and friend, found his wish with El Dorado Holdings on the Nile.

3. The Power of Partnerships

**Bev and Mark Nuessle, great friends and partners, charting new horizons with El Dorado Holdings and cruising the Nile in timeless style.**

## CHAPTER FOUR
## THE POWER OF TEAMWORK

Have you ever met someone who thought they could do it all themselves? They didn't need anyone; they could achieve all of their goals on their own.

I imagine there are some "go it alone" people who don't need the involvement of others in their lives, but I've never personally met any of them. Working with a team toward a specific goal or outcome can be one of the most rewarding experiences any of us can have. Richard Childress of NASCAR fame is clear proof of that.

For this discussion, I'm going to assume that you don't need to be sold on the value of teamwork. Rather, I'm going to offer my thoughts on the attributes of a good team player. I've always looked for four qualities:

1. A Winner's Attitude
2. A Strong Work Ethic
3. Uncompromising Character
4. The Ability to Forgive and Reconcile

### A Winner's Attitude

Everyone who is part of my team today has the attitude of a winner. One of my favorite Zig Ziglar quotes is,

*"Your attitude, not your aptitude, will determine your altitude."*

As far as I'm concerned, the only attitude a real winner

## 4. The Power of Teamwork

can have and display is a positive one. People who exude positive attitudes will "fly higher" than those who don't. That's why I associate with people who find the good in life's experiences, rather than the bad. For me, it's not only a personal matter—it extends to my work relationships.

I recall a wonderful young woman who was at our reception desk for many years. She was very candid with me: she thought that living in another area would offer increased responsibility and greater opportunity and she wanted to move.

I didn't want to hold her back, but I kept challenging her to stay in her position. I said, "You'll be the highest paid front desk person in this town if you realize how important you are in your position. You have a winner's attitude, and it's the first thing people see when they walk through our door."

Her talents, her people skills, her telephone voice, and the ways she greeted people made a powerful impression. When she realized, finally, the great contribution she was making to our company, she agreed to stay. Eventually, we gave her additional administrative work. Everyone soon realized she had a number of responsibilities, not just answering the phone, greeting people, and getting them coffee.

In fact, I think the receptionist position is one of the hardest roles to fill because that person is the first impression your company makes. That impression can be good or bad and may affect any future relationships with your customers. I've adopted the position name "Director of First Impressions." The title actually appears on a sign at the reception desk at my El Dorado office because this position is so valuable. A few years ago, my long-time Director of First Impressions decided she wanted to be a stay-at-home mom and raise a family. She continues to work on projects from home (I don't give up on talent easily), but I honestly thought I'd never be able to replace her.

We were lucky. Ms. Karen Mickalonis walked into our lives at El Dorado and has become yet another perfect "Director of First Impressions." I plan to make sure that "Efficient Karen" remains happy and challenged because I know what an important job she has. I also know how difficult it can be to find that special person who makes the right first impression.

## A Strong Work Ethic

People often ask me why I work so hard. There are two reasons for my dedication to work. First, I have a responsibility toward my investors. If it were only my money involved in all our projects, I guarantee I wouldn't work nearly as hard. But when others invest their money and their trust in me, it puts me in a different place—where I must do my very best. Second, I enjoy the financial rewards. It makes it possible for me to continue to give generously to organizations in which I believe. To quote Zig again, "I've been with money and without it . . . and it's better with it."

My philosophy is simple: *Work Hard and Play Hard*. I believe that the people on my team understand this about me, and they, too, are willing to work hard for the rewards they receive.

## 4. The Power of Teamwork

**Foundations of El Dorado Holdings: Dr. Jim Little—my first partner, Deb Bricker—my right hand from Day Two, and me. A legacy built on trust, vision, and enduring partnerships.**

Right now, I'm thinking about Deb Bricker, one of the smartest and most loyal and dedicated people I've ever encountered. I value her as a partner, a team member, and a trusted friend. Deb has been with El Dorado Holdings exactly one day less than I have. That's since 1987. In fact, Deb has capably served us as a director, my partner, and our Designated Broker, a position that's required within every company working in the field of real estate. I love to tell the story about how our partners used to call and ask to speak to me about their investments. When they figured out I had to ask Deb first, they learned to go directly to her to find out the status and our plans for their investments. She's the

## 4. The Power of Teamwork

over-viewer of all that is El Dorado. I'm reminded of the saying, "Do you want to speak to the man in charge or the woman who knows what's going on?"

Ms. Bricker—and the rest of the great people on my team—will come in early and stay late because they have solid work ethics. They understand the importance of:

- Getting the job done
- Doing the job right
- Meeting or exceeding the customer's expectations

When the people on my team take on an assignment, they're promising me they'll finish it. But I look for more than that. I look for the ones who also attend to the small details. My team gives everything they've got to do the job right. "Whatever it takes" could be their mantra. They realize that customers have legitimate expectations that must be met—or those customers will soon become ex-customers. It all comes down to work ethic. It's an individual trait that people either possess or they don't. I look for the people who do.

They say a college degree indicates that an individual possesses a certain level of dedication and focus. When I'm hiring, I don't look too much at an individual's educational experience; I look at his or her desire to excel. That desire is a key component of their work ethic. Hard work and perseverance usually outweigh a truckload of book smarts.

Evidence seems to show this trait is instilled at a very early age. Deb Bricker has a strong work ethic. In the course of her full-time career with us, she also raised two kids into two exceptional adults. Deb spent a lot of her upbringing

## 4. The Power of Teamwork

in the oil fields of Wyoming. Her mom and dad were hard workers. It ran in the family because Deb's sister (who sadly passed away at far too young an age) was also intelligent and had a strong work ethic. I suspect that trait was taught and modeled in the home.

Jim Kenny in retirement on Cape Cod after leading El Dorado Holdings for many years as President and CEO.

## Uncompromising Character

I've never found a written or oral exam that can help me determine a person's character, yet character is another important thing I look for in a team member.

## 4. The Power of Teamwork

When I sit down with prospects, I always engage in conversation about their background because the past tells a lot about the future. In my mind, I'm asking, "Will the people I'm doing business with—whether it's clients or partners—look at this person and have respect for him or her and realize that this is a person of high integrity?"

This is important, because any person you hire is going to represent you and your values. After I've talked with candidates for a while, I start getting a sense... a gut feeling... about their values, about what's really important to them. Is it more than just a paycheck?

I also notice the innate qualities of people who work for other companies. If someone working for another firm shows obvious character, it's likely it will carry over to a position with my company. That's how I first met Jim Kenny, Linda Cheney, Brad Hinton, and Chris Grogan. I already had a history with them. Take Jim Kenny, who was the CEO of our company until recently retiring. I watched him come up through three other companies with which I enjoyed relationships. I saw how he accepted and welcomed greater responsibility with each of these companies.

Here's a secret tactic I use when I'm looking for new team members: I sometimes seek out people who aren't looking for a change. When I hired Jim Kenny, he wasn't looking for a job. I went to him. After taking over as El Dorado's President and then CEO, Jim was highly sought after to participate in many real estate and economic development organizations. He was a member of Greater Phoenix Leadership, Maricopa Association of Governments, Canada Arizona Business Council, and I-11 Coalition. In addition, he sat on the Board of Directors of WESTMARC, as well as

## 4. The Power of Teamwork

the Arizona Chamber of Commerce, the Valley Partnership, and the Maricopa Economic Development Alliance. Jim's expertise was valuable to these organizations, and in turn, his participation provided El Dorado a "seat at the table" to promote and protect our investments.

Likewise, our retired Senior Vice President, Linda Cheney, was not looking for change. I went to her and presented the opportunity to join El Dorado. Linda's background in engineering and her eye for detail added an extremely valuable component to our team. Like Jim, Linda represented El Dorado in area organizations important to our landholdings, including the Maricopa Stanfield Irrigation & Drainage District and the Pinal Partnership where she was a board member. She was also a member of Valley Partnership, the Lower Santa Cruz River Alliance, and the Home Builders Association of Central Arizona. Her experience has been so valuable to the City of Maricopa, city and county administrators have told me she should be on their payroll.

Brad Hinton, our newest Vice President, previously worked in the planning department for the City of Maricopa. It's an office we deal with frequently because of our many real estate projects there. I'm so pleased Brad is now working as a trusted El Dorado team member and is playing an essential role in planning and developing our major investment properties in Maricopa and elsewhere. I knew all these people and their high standards before I hired them, because I'd had the opportunity to observe them.

El Dorado's accounting office is made up of two women of utmost integrity whose opposite personalities seem to

## 4. The Power of Teamwork

harmonize. Our long-time controller, Janet Stewart, is a serious, unshakable "watcher of the funds," who still takes on numerous special El Dorado assignments, even though she's semi-retired. (We were fortunate to find Al Blasi, our controller, and Chris Canavan, our CFO, to take over for Janet several years ago, and I couldn't be more pleased with how Al has fit into our organization.) In contrast to *serious* Janet, Louise Leland is our bookkeeper. She's a bubbly soul whose delightful laugh can often be heard throughout our office and makes everyone smile. That's why we have designated her our "Director of Humor."

A newer key member of our ever-evolving team is Stephanie Morrison, who heads up the Investor Relations Department and works directly with Deb Bricker to interact with all our partners and keep them informed of their various investments. She also stepped into the role of Designated Broker for our company. There's one more advantage to having Stephanie on our team. Though she and I didn't know it when she started, we discovered she has a talent for the business aspects of raising and training registered quarter horses. What a bonus for me! I love my horse business.

Now let me tell you about Chris Grogan. Back in 2011, I added a young man to our team. It was during some rough economic times, but I'm always in the market for talent. At the time, Chris had a successful real estate career at CB Richard Ellis. But I saw attributes in him that would complement El Dorado, so I convinced Chris to make a change.

After hiring him, I decided Chris should become the "face of El Dorado" in business negotiations and also at

## 4. The Power of Teamwork

events and conventions. Every company that wants to survive long-term needs to add competent, engaged people who can carry it forward into the future. We've given him the title of "Event Planner Extraordinaire" because of his fantastic ability to plan and coordinate investor events. At one investor gathering we hosted in Washington, D.C., Chris arranged for a tour of the Museum of the Bible, a remarkable facility funded by David and Barbara Green, founders of Hobby Lobby.

Chris is also deeply involved in our relationships with our investors, along with searching out new investment opportunities and marketing our established properties. Due to his ability and hard work since he joined our company, I'm proud to add Chris as an El Dorado partner, joining Deb in that position. In 2023, I made him President of El Dorado. Naturally, I'm looking forward to watching him continue to grow and reach his full potential at the company.

Dave Brown came to El Dorado with a great building background in his family. Our first development was a Fry's grocery neighborhood shopping center in the city of Chandler, Arizona. The shopping center was surrounded by a home development we did with his family, called Homes by Dave Brown. Dave Jr., his son, is now President of our Homes for Rent Division, EVR. Dave has now added a very competent and skilled team member, Adam Walter. The two of them have created a strong division for El Dorado.

## The Ability to Forgive and Reconcile

You may not believe me when I tell you this, but I honestly cannot recall a single instance in which someone on our team has spoken an unkind, angry word to another team member. Yes, we have our discussions—our disagreements—but they do not escalate to anything more. Maybe I'm simply blessed to find amazing people with cooperative spirits!

Still, at some point, every team will experience conflict . . . and it may not be pretty. That's where the ability to forgive and reconcile comes into play. I discuss forgiveness in more detail later in the book. But for now, I want to emphasize this simple truth: in a fast-paced, highly competitive business environment, people will sometimes disagree, and occasionally tempers can flare. A true team player will forgive any wrongs for the good of the organization and reconcile as quickly as possible. It takes maturity, personal strength, and positive self-esteem to forgive and move on.

Renowned theologian and author Lewis B. Smedes, once observed,

*"To forgive is to set a prisoner free and discover that the prisoner was you."*

Let me add to that the words of Argentine-born evangelist and author Luis Palau:

*"Forgive and be forgiven. And then forget it. This is the secret of spiritual health. Keep short accounts with God and men. Don't lock bitterness and guilt within the closet of your soul."*

## 4. The Power of Teamwork

When you look at the four characteristics of effective team members—A Winner's Attitude, A Strong Work Ethic, Uncompromising Character, and The Ability to Forgive and Reconcile—it all comes down to one thing for me:

*It's a matter of the heart!*

# CHAPTER FIVE
# THE POWER OF LOYALTY

Some of the greatest illustrations of loyalty, or *lack* of loyalty, can be found in the stories of the life and times of Jesus. It's always been a mystery to me how Jesus went about picking his team. It's as if someone else chose all the "stars," and he took what was left over. One of them, Matthew, was a tax collector whom everyone hated. A couple were smelly fishermen, barely out of their teens. (Not that anyone probably smelled too good in 30 A.D.) One of his top teammates, Peter, denied he even knew Jesus when the going got tough the night of his trial. Another follower, Judas, started the chain of events that led to Jesus' death by trading his spiritual mentor in for a bag of silver coins.

Yet, Peter and most of the others went on to achieve great things, spreading the message of Christianity far and wide, even though doing so involved great sacrifice. They believed in the truths they'd been taught, they'd witnessed unimaginable miracles, and they'd seen real love in action. Their leader was faithful all the way to the cross.

Which brings me to the main point of this chapter. If you want to build loyalty among your team members, you have to be a leader worth following. You may think the points I'm about to make are obvious. You've heard them, seen them, or read them before. Doesn't everyone reading this book already know and apply them?

## 5. The Power of Loyalty

I wish that were true. But I meet leaders all the time who overlook—even forget—many of the basics. In order to gain the loyalty of your team, these are the five most vital habits you must nurture in your personal and business life:

1. **Be Transparent About Who You Are.** *No one is loyal to a phony. Leaders who admit their shortcomings not only gain respect, but they also attract followers who can help them "fill in the blanks."* I've always said to Sheila, "Please don't ever let me become arrogant." She's very good at reminding me. She could keep anyone humble.

2. **Make Your Vision Clear.** *Most leaders have a vision for their lives and organizations, but it's amazing how many of them are unable to articulate that vision.* I believe in telling the team—then reminding them again and again—what my vision is. Understanding my vision is the first step to "buying in," and you need the buy-in of everyone on your team to follow the path you set forth.

3. **Clarify Your Specific Goals.** *Realizing a vision is an ongoing process. Small, easily defined goals are part of the process.* My team and I had a vision for creating a new city in the middle of the desert south of Phoenix. It actually came about. I describe it later in the book. But it was the methodical achievement of each incremental goal that led to the big picture—the vision that became Maricopa, Arizona. As Zig Ziglar pointed out, *"A goal properly set is halfway reached."*

## 5. The Power of Loyalty

4. **Measure Your Progress Toward Those Goals.** *As Harvey MacKay wrote, "A dream is just a dream. A goal is a dream with a plan and a deadline."* Every goal, no matter how small, needs a deadline. By checking both big and little things off your list, you get a better sense of your progress. Few people can see the entire outline of their goal at the beginning. Zig Ziglar once told me, "If you can't see the entire plan, go as far as you can see. When you reach that point, I can guarantee you will be able to see further." You may need to make adjustments along the way, but it doesn't mean you abandon your ultimate goal. According to Zig, some people just do whatever makes them feel good. It's better to be someone with a specific goal. As Paul Harvey used to say, *"Leave the wood pile higher than you found it."*

5. **Acknowledge and Reward Success.** *Nothing discourages a team member more than a lack of appreciation from the leader.* Discouragement destroys loyalty. How can you acknowledge and reward success? The two ways that most team members appreciate are praise and pay increases or bonuses. When someone is both privately and publicly praised and when that praise is followed by a monetary reward, it should be clear to all that the team member's contributions were valued.

## Loyalty is a Two-Way Street

Depending on the business venture I'm involved in, I actively seek and nurture the loyalty of four groups: team

## 5. The Power of Loyalty

members (employees), suppliers, investors, and customers. In the sales and distribution business, I naturally worked with suppliers and manufacturers, while in the land development business, I work with land planners, engineers, and brokers, as well as our investors.

> **When it comes to my team,
> loyalty is a two-way street.**

I mentioned previously that I have told new hires, "You can tear up your resume. I don't think you'll ever be looking for another job again." I make this bold promise because I know enough about people before I hire them. It's clear to me they will be a good fit, so I can commit to meeting their needs for increased earnings and advancement. I knew my assistant, Denise Organ, so well that I would have been stunned had she not become one of my best long-term teammates ever.

Of course, there's a potential downside to this commitment. When the recession began in 2007 and caused tremendous suffering in the Arizona real estate industry, I committed to my team that I wouldn't let anyone go. Everyone understood there'd be no bonuses, no pay raises, and many of the usual "El Dorado Perks" would stop; however, everyone would continue to have a job—period. It also came at a great deal of personal cost. I could no longer entertain investors and promote El Dorado as I had in the past, and my personal income was substantially reduced in order to keep our employees. Looking back, I had to sell a lot of personal assets to keep the company going, but I've never once regretted making that promise.

## 5. The Power of Loyalty

*Our relationship with suppliers
is also a two-way street.*

In real estate, our suppliers are brokers, lawyers, surveyors, architects, and the like. Because our vendors know they'll benefit from new ventures, they're dedicated to giving us both the service and the quality we've come to expect. Meanwhile, we're committed to compensating them fairly and on time.

Come to think of it, our relationship with investors is a two-way street as well. We build our company using their investments, and they expect us to provide a reasonable return on their money. When we deliver, they reward us with their loyalty.

One of our first investors was Dr. Jim Little, a world-famous ophthalmologist from Oklahoma City who pioneered several major surgical procedures. Sadly, Jim passed away in 2023 at the age of 89. He invested in our first venture and, to this day, remains the largest investor we've ever had. Throughout his life, he continued to be involved in every new offering and has brought in many of his friends and colleagues as investors over the years. He even became a shareholder in our management company, El Dorado Holdings. I was happy to offer Jim an ownership position because he stepped up to the table during our early years and provided working capital when we needed it. We both shared the value of loyalty. In fact, Dr. Jim is the perfect model for an investor and a partner. No one could be better. After his death, his daughters remain strong partners with us and one, Jan Bradford, now sits on the Board of Directors replacing her father's seat.

## 5. The Power of Loyalty

When a relationship is working, there's no reason to change it. In fact, true loyalty shows up when a need to change surfaces. The underlying loyalty becomes the glue that helps the relationship survive. I've seen many marriages survive unbearable hardships because loyalty and love held them together. This applies not only to my happy, long-lasting marriage to Sheila, but also to our relationships with investors and team members.

### *How is our relationship with customers a two-way street?*

Customers fit into our company in an odd sort of way. Our actual customers are the homebuilders and commercial developers who buy the land offered by El Dorado Holdings. In the end, however, I believe our customers are the families who buy the homes and the businesses who build or lease commercial space.

To gain the loyalty of homebuilders and commercial developers, we have to deliver on our promises—infrastructure, improvements, amenities, and the like. Loyalty on the part of families involves positive word-of-mouth. When we and the builders deliver on our collective promises, families recommend our developments to their friends. Houses become homes and homes become communities.

Loyalty, indeed, is an essential part of building any successful company.

# CHAPTER SIX
# THE POWER OF TRUST

A man I greatly admire is the late S. Truett Cathy, the founder of Chick-fil-A. He is quoted as saying, *"Success in any relationship or endeavor begins with trust."* I've thought long and hard about this chapter because trust is a difficult thing to understand and explain. I think the reason is that it's so fragile. It can take years to build trust, but the smallest thing can destroy it. Then it takes more years to rebuild it—if it ever *can* be rebuilt.

Think about these two situations: marriage and parenting teenagers. When one of the partners in a marriage strays into an extra-marital relationship, it's almost impossible to restore trust. It takes a lot of time, a lot of counseling, and, I believe, a lot of prayer. It requires an almost supernatural measure of forgiveness. I've never seen an "overnight fix" in this situation, and I've witnessed this sad story unfold in the lives of lots of friends and acquaintances.

Also, if your teenage son or daughter breaks your trust by getting involved with drugs or alcohol or by driving recklessly or by committing some crime, it will invariably take a lot of time to rebuild the relationship. You'll want to believe that things have changed, but it's likely there will always be a nagging doubt.

## 6. The Power of Trust

Of course, the obvious way to gain trust is to be trustworthy. Simple, right? At El Dorado Holdings, we seek to be the trusted source of sound investment opportunities in real estate. We have investors who've signed up for every deal we've ever offered because they know from experience their trust is well-placed.

I had one instance where my desire to instill trust in my investors almost backfired, though. The first time I approached Dr. Little to invest with us was when we put together our first deal. Both of us were busy at the time, so we couldn't meet in person. I called him on the phone and presented the opportunity. He told me, "That sounds great, Mike. I'll take a percentage of that deal."

Deb Bricker stayed up all night long, putting together a nice marketing package for Dr. Little so he could review all the details. He called the next day, reached Deb and said, "I've decided not to go in on this offering after all."

Confused, I called him back and asked, "Jim, what's wrong? Why don't you want to invest in this project?"

He responded, "You've obviously shopped this all over the country, and you've probably come to me as a last resort."

"Why do you say that?" I asked.

"Well, you sent me this slick marketing package, so I'm guessing you've presented it far and wide."

I almost choked on that one. "No, Jim," I said, "you're the first and only person I've presented this to. Deb stayed up all night long to put together a package so you would have an idea of what you were getting into."

## 6. The Power of Trust

"Oh, okay," he replied. "Well, in that case, yeah, put me in. In fact, I'll double my investment." And he did.

I learned something about trust from that experience. People have different ideas of what it means to trust and be trusted. Dr. Little, like so many of our investors since then, wanted to be in on the ground floor. His trust results from being "in the know" right from the start. Believe it or not, many of our most successful ventures have their beginnings in restaurants, drawn out on paper napkins. That's because paper napkins look like the ground floor, and our investors trust that!

### Larry Williams

Larry Williams is an early partner of mine and now a trusted friend. It took a while for Larry to get to that point of trust with me. I'll let him tell you about it in his own words:

*I was introduced to Mike many years ago through a good friend of mine, Jerry Caven. Jerry had started investing with Mike and had done quite well.*

*At first, I was quite skeptical as Mike seemed to be just too good a salesman. It took me several years to figure out that he was for real. I cautiously started investing in Mike's deals and found out that Jerry was right; this guy could make deals happen. After three or four years of making some nice returns and getting comfortable with Mike, I started getting some other people (including some of my employees) into Mike's investments.*

*In 1999, when Mike put together investors for the Circle Cross Ranch property, I made a big commitment as I thought we had our company sold (which didn't occur). I talked to Mike*

## 6. The Power of Trust

*about reducing our portion down, but being the super salesman that he is, Mike talked me into staying in for the full amount.*

*When I finally saw the property several months later, I was scared to death. It was literally in the middle of nowhere, and to top it off, we were going to have to demo a huge feedlot. Fortunately, Mike saw something there that I certainly didn't, and it ended up being the best investment we ever made! Today, we are all very appreciative of our involvement with Mike. It has been a very profitable thirty-plus years for all of us.*

*Mike and I not only became business partners, but also good friends. We rodeo, hunt, boat, and just generally have a great time together. My wife and I always enjoy spending time with Mike and Sheila.*

*Mike always contributes more than his fair share in whatever he does. Here's to another twenty years!*

**With some of my partners in Bell Cross Ranch, Dave Kingston, me, Robin Sorensen, Larry Williams, and Shon Craig.**

You might guess that one key to building trust is to build a relationship first. We all tend to have low levels of

## 6. The Power of Trust

trust for people we don't know well. Because I enjoy rodeo, hunting, fishing, golf, and many other outdoor activities, I naturally attract investors who have similar interests. I use these shared interests to build relationships. From my days in wholesale distributing to today, I plan activities that include investors or even potential investors. That's how they get to know me. It becomes the first step to earning their trust. I haven't missed a year taking a group with me to the National Finals Rodeo, and for the past forty years, I've organized fishing trips to either Alaska or British Columbia, with fifty or sixty investors. We've also booked many pheasant hunting trips to the great state of South Dakota and Oregon. In the process, we raised money for great charities including the Gary Sinise Foundation, Navy Seal Foundation, Wounded Warrior Project, and the Joe Foss Institute, which promotes civic education programs for youth groups and public school students.

As I'm sure you well know, people buy from people they know, trust, and respect, people with whom they have relationships. In fact, it's known that people who give to a particular charity often do so because of the individual who leads that charity. They believe in and invest in the individual who is leading that cause. In my opinion, they give to the person, who then validates the cause and mission.

### Gary Sinise

Take Gary Sinise, for example, a celebrated actor who appeared in many movies, including *Forrest Gump,* and the hit TV series, *CSI:NY.* In 2003, he formed the Lt. Dan Band to perform at USO shows, to entertain troops, and to raise

## 6. The Power of Trust

money for disabled veterans. The band is named after the character Lieutenant Dan Taylor, whom Gary portrayed in the film *Forrest Gump*.

**With Gary Sinise — a tireless advocate for our veterans and a true American Patriot on his very first hunt.**

Touched by the tragic events of September 11, 2001, Gary has also devoted his time to supporting the brave men and women who responded to those attacks. In 2011, he established the Gary Sinise Foundation "to support our nation's defenders, veterans, first responders and their loved ones." The Foundation's First Responders Outreach program "provides funding for emergency relief, training, and essential equipment to ensure these heroes perform to the best of their abilities." And for those severely wounded

## 6. The Power of Trust

in the line of duty, they build "100% mortgage-free, specially adapted smart homes as well as providing home modifications, mobility devices, and adapted vehicles." Please go to the foundation for more information and to make a donation: https://www.garysinisefoundation.org.

In 2012, Gary was made an honorary U.S. Navy Chief Petty Officer. In 2013, he was named an honorary Marine by the Commandant of the Marine Corps and, that same year, he received the third highest honor from the Department of the Army Civilian Awards, the Outstanding Civilian Service Award. Is it a surprise that I see him as a trusted leader? My trust in him—combined with my trust in the purpose, validity, and integrity of his causes—made it easy for me to become a loyal, long-term supporter of these fine organizations.

### Be the Leader You Seek

I strive to be the leader that others can trust as well. There was one trip, though, where I thought I was going to lose the trust of my investors forever. I took thirty of our investors to the Amazon River on a bass fishing and hunting trip. The month of February is usually a dry season in the Amazon, but this particular year, they had the worst rain and floods they'd ever had. The Amazon was running about fourteen to eighteen feet above flood stage.

To get to the lodge, we had to travel up the river in open bass boats. By the time we got to our destination, our luggage was soaked and so were we. Humidity was hovering around a hundred percent, and it was very difficult, if not impossible, to get anything to dry out.

## 6. The Power of Trust

Undaunted, we were ready to go fishing the next morning. Then the manager told us he had a problem—all his fishing guides had gone on strike. The next day we found ourselves sitting around the lodge, playing cards and telling stories. They finally found guides to take us fishing, but we didn't catch a lot of fish because the water was so high.

Out fishing one day, we stopped on the shore for lunch. When we returned to our boat, we discovered it was taking on water—but only after we left the shore and started to sink! Even worse, we didn't have any life jackets. Now, the Amazon River is so wide we could look in both directions and not see the shore. Did you know that 20% of all the fresh water in the world comes out of the mountains and into the Amazon? I do now.

We were in a frightening situation, especially for my wife, Sheila, who can't swim. Did I mention there were piranhas in the water? Poor Sheila. There she was, trying to dip water out of the boat with a Coke bottle. The guide was in the back, bailing water with a cup. But it was filling up faster than they could bail. We were praying for help and trying to control our rising panic. At last, another boat came along, and the crew threw us some life jackets and pulled us back to shore.

What a trip! It rained almost every day. Our guides were on strike. We caught very few fish. We always wore wet clothes (thanks to the humidity), and our boat nearly sank.

When we got ready to leave, we were told the only airline that services that part of Brazil, Bolivian Airlines, was also on strike. Once again, with the mantra, "Whatever

## 6. The Power of Trust

it takes," we regrouped and called in a charter service from the United States to come pick us up.

You'd think it was the worst trip imaginable and that my thirty investors would never trust me again. In reality, it left such an indelible memory that we had T-shirts printed up saying, "Everything Strikes in the Amazon Except the Bass!"

To this day, our investors—whom I refer to as partners—say it was one of the greatest trips we'd ever had because we all got to know each other so well and our relationships were strengthened.

Some people doubt that this sort of trust-building adventure can actually succeed. A good friend of mine who's in the development business ran into me and a group of my investors as we were checking into a hotel in Vancouver ahead of a salmon fishing adventure. The first words out of his mouth? "Mike, what on earth are you doing? Bringing your investors together is a formula for disaster. I'd never get more than two of my investors together at any one time."

"Well, you know," I replied, "that's just a difference in philosophy. I get the greatest joy out of bringing our investors together. We share stories, we learn from one another, and a lot of them have become great friends. I don't plan it that way; it just works out that way. Our investors love to associate with other successful people."

Basically, trust is at the core of my relationship with my investors, so I have no fear of bringing them together. Everything about our partnerships is open. And because our partnerships are structured in such a way that I can be

### 6. The Power of Trust

removed from my management role at any time, I make sure to perform at all times. And performance leads to trust.

## A Great Lesson in Being Trustworthy

I had the pleasure of meeting Alphonso Jackson at the 2018 Horatio Alger Award ceremony where he was being inducted. Alphonso was the 13th U.S. Secretary of Housing and Urban Development (HUD), nominated by President George W. Bush in 2004, serving until 2008. Alphonso started his career as an assistant professor at the University of Missouri and since has taken on many roles in both the private and public sectors, including Executive Director of the St. Louis Housing Authority, Director of the U.S. Department of Public and Assisted Housing in Washington, D.C. and President and CEO of the Housing Authority of the City of Dallas. After leaving his position as U.S. Secretary of HUD, Alphonso returned to the private sector to become Vice Chairman of Consumer and Community Banking with JP Morgan Chase. I was so impressed by the man and his life accomplishments.

During the Horatio Alger event, Alphonso told me of a powerful quote he's used many times by the Reverend Dr. Cecil "Chip" Murray. The quote really meant a lot to me, and I hope I handle all of my personal and business dealings in this manner. Rev. Murray said, *"Talk without being offensive, listen without being defensive, and always leave even your adversary with their dignity."*

I hope I handle all of my personal and business dealings in this manner.

# CHAPTER SEVEN
# THE POWER OF CUSTOMERS

Of all the "people relationships" I've talked about, your relationship with your customers is potentially the most volatile. Why? You need your customers, but they may not need you. Chances are they can get what they want from someone else. It's the nature of our competitive economy.

The people who invest their money with El Dorado Holdings, for example, have several other options. They can invest in stocks and bonds, in certificates of deposit, in precious metals, in oil and gas exploration, in foreign currencies, in residential/commercial real estate or rental properties, or with other companies similar to El Dorado. They can even invest in Hollywood films and theatrical productions.

The customers who buy our land—the homebuilders and developers—need to make a profit because of buying it, building on it, and selling it to their customers. Those customers also have choices. They can buy existing homes or condos, they can choose to buy in other neighborhoods, or they can rent an apartment or house.

I've discovered over the years that customers want four basic things, no matter what they're buying:

1. A quality product
2. A competitive price

3. A warranty that is supported
4. Excellent customer service

I talk about the importance of a quality product in more depth later in the book. But what about the other three basic "wants?"

## The Other Three "Wants"

There's always a delicate balance between attracting a customer through price and still making a profit on the transaction. I once heard a radio commercial for a car dealer in which the promise was, "We lose a little on every deal, but we make it up on volume." The promise may actually work for a car dealer, because car dealers generally make most of their money in the service department and on holdback bonuses. But in the real world where most businesses operate, this is absolutely absurd. If a company loses a little on every deal, they'll lose *a lot* on volume.

Here's where the "magic" of these four "customer wants" comes into play. If you're not offering a quality product, you will likely not stay in business, unless the product you're selling has no viable competition in your market. That's why a really crummy airline can survive and charge outrageous fares, if it's the only one flying into a small city.

Even if you offer a quality product, you likely will have to compete on price. But why, then, do some costly alternatives succeed—like Apple computers—you ask? I promise to take that mystery up in the next chapter.

Let's say your product isn't that much different from that of your competitors. If your price point is typical for

# 7. The Power of Customers

the category, how do you gain a competitive edge with your potential customers? The answer is found in the last two customer wants: a warranty that is supported and excellent customer service.

I personally know people who have the money to buy any Mercedes-Benz, BMW, Jaguar, or Cadillac that catches their eye. But instead, they buy a Hyundai because of the manufacturer's bold ten-year warranty and the support with which they back it up. Of course, if your plan is to lease or own your car for only three or four years, a ten-year warranty becomes less relevant. Excellent customer service now becomes more significant.

**Wes Adams and Dave Kingston, partners with me in the 8,700-acre Bell Cross Ranch, outside of Great Falls, MT.**

My long-time investor and friend, Wes Adams, whom we unfortunately lost in February 2011, often said, "In any conversation, someone is selling and someone is being sold." In any transaction, a successful outcome is based on trust and mutual respect. The party being sold has to respect the seller in order to become a customer. And the seller must earn that respect.

The bottom line is that your customers are the key to your success. It takes a careful balance of these four components to attract them, keep them happy, and retain them.

If companies expended as much energy in making sure their current customers were happy as they do in trying to attract new customers, they'd experience much greater success. My belief is that customer and investor retention is 75% of the secret to our company's success.

# THE SECOND KEY: PRODUCT POWER

## CHAPTER EIGHT
# THE POWER OF INNOVATION

As you well know, several books have been written about the creative genius of the late Steve Jobs, one of the original founders of Apple, who was forced out of power in the 1980s, but who made his triumphant return in the 1990s to rescue the company from the brink of demise.

Steve was not an expert on computers, and he might not have been the nicest guy who ever lived. I would not want to emulate all of his approaches to business and to life. But he *was* gifted with the power of innovative thinking. There were already MP3 players on the market when he guided the design of the iPod. But none was as elegant, aesthetically pleasing, or as easy to use. There were already scores of cellular phones on the market when the iPhone was released. But none so capable, so feature-rich, or again, so aesthetically pleasing. There were already tablet computers, but none as highly functioning as the iPad, thanks in part to the hundreds of thousands of apps that had already been created for the iPhone and iPod Touch.

There are, I believe, three opportunities for innovation that every individual and every company need to explore:

**1.** It's never been done.
**2.** It's already been done, but not as well as it could be.

## 8. The Power of Innovation

    **3.** It's already been done well, but not as inexpensively or as efficiently as it could have been.

Think about the key words that have been employed in so many marketing campaigns: "NEW," "IMPROVED," "PRICE REDUCED," "ON SALE NOW." If you're an Apple user you know that Steve Jobs, Tim Cook, and their associates never developed anything totally new, while their prices have never been lowest in the market. Most PC laptops cost about half as much as a comparable Apple MacBook. Think about it. Steve and company excelled on the second key element of innovation: "It's already been done, but not as well as it could have been."

Many people who experience the Macintosh Operating System (iOS) wonder why the Microsoft OS can't be as straightforward, intuitive, and crash-resistant. The answer is simple: They didn't "copy" Microsoft. They innovated. In fact, it could easily be argued that Microsoft has copied Apple.

### Southwest Airlines

Here's another example of innovative thinking: Back in 1971, the late Herb Kelleher started Southwest Airlines. He had some interesting ideas on how to get business travelers hooked on his airline by setting it apart from the pack. For starters, he ran an airline that was on time and dependable. Also, he offered low fares that blew away the competition. Plus, Southwest Airlines' "bags fly free"—and still do.

But there were other things that Herb relied on to set his airline apart. He built a culture of friendly, cheerful personnel, people who were accommodating, and gave

## 8. The Power of Innovation

you the feeling they appreciated your business. And it was real. Do you want to fly with somebody who acts as though they're doing you a favor? Or would you rather stick with somebody who lets you know they value your business and appreciate the fact that you're flying with them? It didn't take long for Southwest Airlines to move to the top of the pack because people love to feel they're valued.

I've flown Southwest Airlines countless times, and I appreciate them. Nowadays, when you call most major airlines for a reservation, you have to hit too many buttons and enter too many codes, hoping that you'll finally get to talk to a human being. That's not the case with Southwest. Just stay on the line for a few moments, and you'll talk to a real person . . . an actual human being who will help you.

From counter people to gate agents to baggage handlers, they're all friendly, helpful professionals. Both Sheila and I feel such appreciation for the personnel at Southwest, we organized a huge barbeque for them at our Paradise Valley home and invited the entire Phoenix crew. A lot of them attended, including gate personnel, baggage handlers, and even pilots. Many of my El Dorado staff also came to show their appreciation for these fine people.

Even though they've grown, they still maintain that personal touch. Southwest Airlines never worried about doing something that hadn't been done before. Instead, they wisely focused on the other keys to innovation: not just doing it better, but doing it cheaper and more efficiently. As long as they stick to those two plans, they'll continue to be a standout in the industry.

## 8. The Power of Innovation

My long-time friends and partners,
Dr. Jim Little and his wife, Margaret.

### Jim Little

I've got to mention my friend, Jim Little, again. Without Jim, I don't know how El Dorado Holdings would've gotten off the ground. I met Jim through his wife when I was in business back in Oklahoma. Margaret came into our place to buy veterinary supplies. She and Jim had a place about a mile west of our warehouse and they kept horses. I explained to Margaret that we didn't sell retail, but she persisted. "Don't you have any damaged products you can't sell?" she asked. When I admitted we did, she asked if she could see if there was anything she could use. I'm thinking this woman had a unique approach, so I took her back to the shelf that held

## 8. The Power of Innovation

the damaged products. "Oh, I could use some of this" and "I could take some of that," she said. Before I knew it, she'd picked up a bunch of damaged products, all with a big-time discount.

It wasn't long before I met Jim and his family. Although he always called himself Jim, I should refer to him as Dr. Little because he practiced ophthalmology in Oklahoma City for forty years. But Jim was no ordinary doctor. His specialty was cataract surgeries. Now, you need to know that, before the 1970s, cataracts required large incisions to surgically remove them. That often led to patients being hospitalized for several days, and it wasn't unusual for the surgeries to lead to astigmatism. Jim Little believed that a smaller incision would be an improvement.

When Jim met Dr. Charles D. Kelman, he knew he was on the right track. The New York doctor had discovered a technique called phacoemulsification (don't ask me to pronounce it) that used ultrasonic waves to break up a cataract and suction the fragments out of the eye. The best part was that the technique required an incision a fraction of the size of the old one. That meant less chance of astigmatism and patients could walk out right after the procedure. Jim brought the technique back to Oklahoma.

Over the years, Jim taught it to ophthalmologists all around the world. He also continued to modify the machine and handpiece used for the procedure. His innovations, which are still used today, not only improved on the technique, but they also made him a lot of money. Jim got some pushback from the medical community at first, but his success couldn't be denied. He said that he probably did

## 8. The Power of Innovation

about 50,000 cataract surgeries using the technique during the years he practiced. That's the power of innovation.

### El Dorado Holdings

What about El Dorado Holdings? How do the principles of innovation apply to my business? Over time, I've concluded that for land developers, all three aspects of innovation come into play.

El Dorado Holdings had its beginnings in 1987 with one escrow property south of Phoenix. It happened to be one of the ranches that the famous actor John Wayne owned for over forty-two years—the El Dorado Ranch. As you know by now, I was averse to bank debt, so I raised the money to close on the property through investors. My new company was off and running ... or so I thought.

Within a year of my great purchase, the real estate market in Phoenix started to flounder. I was worried that I wouldn't survive the downturn and would lose all my investors' money. El Dorado had been founded on a wing and a prayer, so we did not have much in the way of reserves. Without sales, our rapidly diminishing coffers would soon be empty. Our telephones quit ringing, and when we called other companies with which we did business—consultants, brokers, engineers, surveyors, and so on—many times we were greeted by that automated reply, "This number is no longer in service." Companies, especially those involved with real estate, were going under in record numbers.

But thankfully, another thing happened in the late 80s that helped me not only weather the downturn but create new opportunities for my company. I discovered the

## 8. The Power of Innovation

Resolution Trust Corporation (RTC), the government entity formed to manage the failed bank and savings and loan institutions.

The RTC *managed* them by selling off their assets at incredible discounts to value. I was fortunate. I'd gathered a group of investors who shared my belief that Phoenix could weather this storm. Because they stuck with me, I was able to buy properties at astoundingly low prices through the RTC.

One of those investors was Dalton Knauss, who was a loyal El Dorado investor until his death. Dalton started his career in his garage, working on electronics. He built his small undertaking into a successful business and ultimately sold his company to Square D. I remember clearly Dalton telling me back then, "Mike, you got this buying down, but when are you going to learn to sell?" I told him there was a time to buy and a time to sell. Thank goodness, a time to sell came along. Dalton's son, Bill, continues to be a valuable investor with El Dorado.

Many of our investments made a profit almost immediately, taking the pressure off the need to make money right away on El Dorado Ranch. For us, innovation meant finding ways to protect the investments we'd made in El Dorado by making substantial new investments during a time of economic decline.

### How to Innovate
- Use innovative ideas to solve a need.
- Employ innovative customer service to build loyalty and repeat business.
- Apply innovative plans to add value.

## 8. The Power of Innovation

That last technique turned out to be essential when it came to developing our properties. In fact, innovation is vital to the advancement of anyone's vision and effectiveness, whether it helps pastors and rabbis communicate with their congregations, or teachers with their students, or even parents with their children. At El Dorado, our innovative ideas created affordable communities with added perks—places people would want to call home.

I believe most people who want to do a better job and create better products and services become innovators. They just need to find the right leaders to guide and motivate the rest of the team to work on those innovative ideas and turn them into reality.

### The Arizona Diamondbacks

When I think about innovation, my association with the Arizona Diamondbacks baseball team comes to mind. About twenty-five years ago, their organization approached the El Dorado partners—at the time, Dr. Jim Little, Monty Ortman, and me—about investing in the ball club. Dr. Little was hesitant because he lives in Oklahoma and wouldn't be able to attend many games. But being a team player, he said, "Mike, if you and Monty want to do this, count me in."

We took the Diamondbacks up on their offer. However, not one of us did so thinking it would be a great investment in terms of any monetary return on our dollars invested. We did it because we believed the Diamondbacks team was important for the state of Arizona and the quality of life for its residents. When promoting the Phoenix area, we could proudly say, at the time, we had four major league sports teams—representing the National Football League (NFL), National Hockey League (NHL), National Basketball Association (NBA), and Major League Baseball (MLB). Not many cities can boast that fact.

The Diamondbacks are an expansion team, voted into the National League in 1998. It can take years for a new sports franchise to become popular with fans. But President Derrick Hall's innovative ideas swiftly built fan loyalty, sponsorship, and involvement. They were the quickest expansion team in MLB history to capture the sport's highest honor, the World Series.

**Celebrating a historic victory: Sheila and me with Jerry Colangelo and the 2001 Arizona Diamondbacks World Series Championship trophy.**

One of my great joys in life was being there for all seven games of the 2001 World Series. The Diamondbacks, with two great pitchers—Randy Johnson and Curt Schilling—won the first two games in Phoenix, then travelled to New York City only to lose all three games there. They returned

## 8. The Power of Innovation

home down three to two. They won the sixth game easily, but game seven came down to the last inning. At the bottom of the ninth, Luis ("Gonzo") Gonzalez hit a blooper to win.

Even today, you can find these words as part of the Arizona Diamondbacks' mission: ". . . to provide industry-leading entertainment in a clean, safe, and family-friendly environment, and to make a positive impact on its fans and civic partners by focusing on team performance, fan experience, financial efficiency, workplace culture, and community contribution." Many thanks to Jerry Colangelo, managing partner through the team's formative years. With his vision and management abilities, he put together a great organization.

My final words on the importance of innovation in your business: If you're not the Steve Jobs within your organization or someone who swings a great bat, it's important that you find the right leader. Every company needs an innovator, whether it's an internal person, a group, an outside consultant or a consulting firm. Innovation is the first step in creating a product or a service that stands out from the crowd. The next couple of chapters will explain how El Dorado used innovative ideas to add value to one community.

## CHAPTER NINE
# THE POWER OF DESIGN

Most people can tell the difference between good design and poor design. Between beautiful and ugly. Between useful and useless. Between well-crafted and poorly made.

For many years, the standard in automobile design and manufacturing was set by foreign competitors—Mercedes-Benz, Toyota, Honda, BMW, Volvo, and the like. They won their reputations based on design, quality, and endurance, not to mention resale value.

These days, American automobile manufacturers have recaptured the greatness they once had. I'm proud to drive my brand new, American-designed-and-built vehicles. If you want to take my pickup truck away from me, you'll have to pry my cold, dead fingers off the steering wheel! I can't tell you what a kick I get when I pull my big, white, Ford F-250 diesel up to some fancy restaurant or event, among the Bentleys, BMWs, and Mercedes, and all the valets fight over who gets to park my truck!

For me, and for most car, truck, and sport utility vehicle buyers, it comes down to the basic elements of design. It has to be:
- Beautiful
- Useful
- Efficient/economical
- Well-made

## 9. The Power of Design

At the core of all this is a simple idea: good design creates value. I define value as "a fair price paid for a quality product, supported by great customer service." Standards are set and those standards are met. There are three kinds of customers engaged in the free enterprise system:

1. Those who get less than they pay for.
2. Those who get exactly what they pay for.
3. Those who get more than they pay for.

The true power of design—and therefore, the power of value—allows us, whether we're individuals or companies, to join the third group, the one that expects and receives more than we pay for. We should also give our customers more than they expect or pay for.

As I mentioned in the last chapter, our first investment in the Phoenix area was in a large parcel of land owned by the legendary John Wayne. The name of his ranch, El Dorado, is what led to the name of our company. It was located just south of the small, unincorporated town of Maricopa, which, at the time, was a mere dot on the map, surrounded by cotton fields and cacti.

Shortly after that purchase, we also bought John Wayne's adjacent property, Red River Ranch. Next, we purchased several farms just north of Maricopa. We decided to focus on developing the northern properties first because they were closer to Interstate 10 and Phoenix itself, with its growing southern suburbs. Our development became known as Rancho El Dorado.

Now, this will sound contradictory, but although this land was useful as farmland, it was basically useless for development. It was in the middle of nowhere, surrounded

## 9. The Power of Design

by parched desert, and had poor access and no services or utilities. However, we knew we could transform it into something beautiful, useful, and just right for a specific purpose. We knew that, through the power of design, we could transform this farmland into an attractive, desirable residential community.

We also knew we needed a great team leader to head up the project. We turned to Mike Reinbold. Mike had a tremendous amount of experience in development. He was able to see the vision we had because he'd worked on similar projects in Southern California. He was the right person at the right time to join our team and make our vision a reality and a huge success. In addition to understanding our vision, Mike had the ability to accept any challenge thrown at him. He still does. I've never heard him say, "This can't be done." It's always, "This is how we're going to get this done."

We announced our plan, and people laughed. The media mocked us. The handful of residents in Maricopa thought we were out of our collective heads. The newspaper reported that we planned to build a residential area, miles from the city proper, and miles from a real freeway. No one believed it would work. But I did, my team did, and our investors did.

The first challenge we faced was the road—or the lack of a road. The tiny town of Maricopa was served by a narrow, two-lane county road that was poorly maintained. You could access from an exit off Interstate 10 between Phoenix and Tucson. It served as a shortcut to Interstate 8 and San Diego. Several miles after taking this exit, drivers passed through Maricopa, a town that boasted little more than a

## 9. The Power of Design

restaurant, a couple of churches, a couple bars, and a small public Arizona school. Fewer than 500 residents called it home. In fact, there was no local government, no mayor, no city council, no police department, and only a small volunteer fire department. There wasn't even a gas station, let alone a hospital or shopping center.

We decided we needed to create a *real* road—four lanes wide—between the freeway exit and the town. It was a daunting task for several reasons, not the least of which was having to deal with and gain cooperation from eight separate groups: private, city, county, state, federal government, and numerous Native American tribal organizations.

To gather support from the private sector, two prominent local farmers, Bill Scott and John Smith, were instrumental in helping me form the Maricopa Road Association. We also gained the support of Donovan Kramer, Sr., publisher of the *Casa Grande Dispatch*, the only local newspaper to service this area. The Maricopa Road Association was made up of local residents who were concerned about the road's safety. Without the hard work of these dedicated people, my role would have been more difficult.

We had great community leadership behind the road project: Supervisor Dean Weatherly of Pinal County; Supervisor Tom Freestone of Maricopa County; Tom White, Cecil Antone, and Mary Thomas of the Gila River Indian Community; Delia Carlyle and Leona Kakar of the Ak-Chin Indian Community; Charlie Miller of the Arizona Department of Transportation; U.S. Senator Dennis DeConcini, and scores of private citizens. Key state legislators, including Senator Alan Stephens and Representatives Jim Hartdegen and

## 9. The Power of Design

Henry Evans, offered support as well. We also had a great deal of opposition, including the Maricopa Association of Governments, Phoenix newspapers, and the chairman of the Arizona Department of Transportation. Any one of these individuals or groups could have single-handedly killed the John Wayne Parkway/State Route 347.

After years of hard work and endless meetings, we reached an agreement, broke ground in 1989, and started building the road to Maricopa in 1990. The media hated it! They referred to it as "The Road to Nowhere."

I'm reminded of something my friend and a man I much admire, T. Boone Pickens, was told by his dad when young Boone was floundering in college. *"A fool with a plan can achieve more than a genius with no plan."* The media thought we at El Dorado Holdings were fools, but we had a plan, and we accomplished what we set out to do. The road was completed in 1996, and that's when things began to change!

The next step was to design the kind of community we believed families would want to call home. We knew we had a competitive edge in pricing, because home sites in this remote area could be sold for much less than lots that were within or closer to the greater Phoenix area. Our design plan included parks, hiking trails, a golf course, recreational facilities, and land set aside for commercial ventures, schools, and public buildings. This plan became Rancho El Dorado, the first master-planned community in Pinal County.

We were lucky we had good people behind the plan. Alma Farrell, who owned a restaurant in Maricopa and also served as the superintendent of the small K–12 school, got

## 9. The Power of Design

solidly behind us, as did her son, Edward. They began the process of incorporating the town as a city, and Edward served as its first mayor. He continued to serve on the city council for many years after that. Tony Smith and Christian Price were two other Maricopa mayors who stood with us and supported our plans. Eventually, the city brought on a very skilled city manager, Rick Horst. He had vision and people skills. With the help of a great city council and mayor, they made the small town into a dynamic and growing city. Tony Smith, Christian Price, and Nancy Smith have been incredible leaders to continue the vision we had hoped for.

All the elements of good design came together in Rancho El Dorado. It was beautiful, it was useful, it was efficient and economical, and it was well made. The families who purchased new homes in Maricopa knew they were benefiting from the power of design.

Our critics may have had a field day early in the process, but as the "Road to Nowhere" began to lead to somewhere, the ridicule gradually died away. A fool with a solid Master Plan—and a good design—had won them over. Maricopa, Arizona, a town of 500 just twenty-odd years ago, has grown into a community of about 75,000 residents. It even survived the "subprime crash" of the 2007–2008 era. Banner Health Hospital, Central Arizona College, three shopping areas, numerous restaurants, and several grocery stores—including a Walmart—are open and thriving. In addition, Home Depot and Lowes are under construction and a new high school recently opened.

Our next task in this unfolding story of design and transformation was to "add value."

9. The Power of Design

The ribbon cutting and ceremonial cake lighting to celebrate the completion of SR 347 (Maricopa Road).

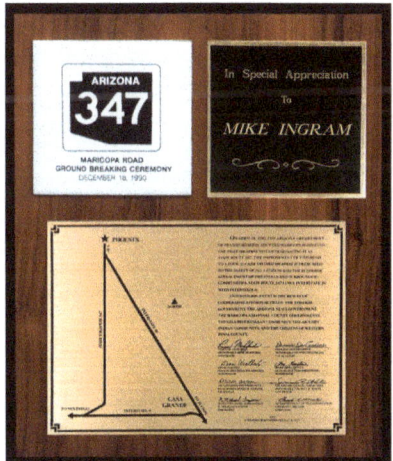

Plaque received at the official groundbreaking of SR 347 (Maricopa Road), December 18, 1990.

Plaque received at the opening of SR 347 (Maricopa Road), May 31, 1996.

## CHAPTER TEN
# THE POWER OF ADDING VALUE

The concept of adding value is simple: Take something good and make it better. Make it worth more, whether it's real worth or actual worth.

With the "Road to Nowhere" completed, we could implement our plans and designs. That's when Mike Reinbold's talent began to add value. The Master Plan called for all sorts of value-added features: main corridors lined with majestic palm trees, attractive street lighting, underground utility service, curbs and gutters, golf courses, and other features.

Our objective was to create an attractive, desirable, affordable suburban community. We knew we couldn't adopt the standards evident in the most luxurious parts of Scottsdale or Palm Desert or Beverly Hills. Yet, we wanted to make sure that our new development in Maricopa was comparable to what you might see within an upscale development in the Southeast Valley of Phoenix, such as Chandler, Mesa, and Gilbert.

We'd toured other recent developments in outlying areas and made a list of things they, in our opinion, had done poorly. One particular community had open carports attached to the houses. We demanded that our builders include a minimum of a two-car garage in all their plans—no carports.

## 10. The Power of Adding Value

That same community allowed composite shingle roofs; we insisted that all roofs be tile. They permitted rooftop-mounted heating and cooling units, a much cheaper way to install the units. We insisted that all units be at ground level and concealed by fencing.

Another community we checked out had a golf course, but it wasn't a championship-style golf course. It didn't have the lighting or the landscaping. Many of the streets weren't paved, there were no sidewalks, and the setbacks from the street were not as great as what we had planned. Also, the building codes were not strict.

We held our builders to a higher standard. Some of them said, "Guys, we want to build one-thousand-square-foot homes or less."

We said, "No home can be smaller than 1,400 square feet." These were the same standards you could see in Chandler or Gilbert, two suburbs of Phoenix. Their standards were higher than those required by the county. Today, the city of Maricopa's standards are as stringent as those of any community in the Phoenix area. It was these standards that added value for homeowners.

### Bringing In Utilities

How else did we add value to the new community? We created partnerships with organizations that provided key services: electricity, cable TV, fiber optics phone service, and transportation. Without these essential partnerships, we wouldn't have had any customers, and we wouldn't have a vibrant community today.

## 10. The Power of Adding Value

The first infrastructure problem we encountered was to provide electrical power. No one wanted to work with us. The big players thought it wouldn't be economically feasible. In their defense, they had no idea that we intended to transform this sleepy community of 500 into a thriving minimetropolis of 200,000 or more. By 2019, Maricopa's estimated population was 50,024, according to the most recent United States census information—estimated to be around 75,000 in 2025!

Because neither Arizona Public Service nor any other of the big utility companies showed any interest in servicing this area, we developed a new electrical power utility. It was in cooperation with Southern California Edison and Electric District 3 (ED3), a rural electric cooperative. For years, local farmers had secured more than adequate power from ED3. As farming had scaled back, however, more than enough power could be made available for this new community.

In cooperation with Edison, we went into the electrical power business. Edison had the capital and knowledge, while ED3 had cheap hydroelectric power—from the Hoover Dam, for example—that they had contracted years ago to meet the farmers' needs. Because those needs had dwindled, they were able to convert that power to residential, commercial, and industrial customers in our new development.

Today, the big power companies probably regret their decision not to service us. They weren't willing to beef up their capacity because they believed that our project would quickly go bankrupt, and the risk was too great.

## 10. The Power of Adding Value

We faced a similar situation with water and wastewater. No existing utility was willing to serve us, so we had to start our own water and wastewater company. It was the same with cable TV service. The local provider, Cox, chose not to provide service, so we partnered with a company called Orbitel Communications to bring cable TV service to our community.

Once all of these utilities were secured, we started digging. We buried all the pipes and cables and brought them to the lot lines so that builders could connect to the new homes they were selling. Without all this value-added effort, the 1,100 home lots that were in escrow could never have been sold and built upon. After a time, another utility company approached us and offered to buy out our utility services company. I'd never wanted to be in the utility business in the first place, so I sold it to them for a very nice profit.

### Adding Rail Service

I didn't want to be in the railroad business, either. But it became apparent that we could add more value to our developments if we offered Amtrak rail service. At the time, service to central Phoenix was going to be shut down, and the closest train station was an old, abandoned one in Casa Grande, twice as far from Phoenix as Maricopa.

In our effort to continue adding value to our community, we formed a public/private partnership with Pinal County back in 2000. But first, we had to find the money for the rail project. I put up some of the money to fund it, and Pinal County also put money into the project. But most of it came

## 10. The Power of Adding Value

from a federal grant we discovered. Brad Gair, the Pinal County Public Works Director, and the Pinal County Board of Supervisors, helped us get the funds put in place, and our own Deb Bricker guided the project with their help. We then sought (and found) the support we needed to locate the Phoenix terminal for Amtrak in Maricopa. To this day, if you want to take the train to or from Phoenix, you board Amtrak in the City of Maricopa.

We wanted to add a little *creative value*, so we found an old California Zephyr sleeping car in Indianapolis. We purchased it, transported it to Chicago, where we had it beautifully refurbished, and then moved it by rail to Maricopa. That refurbished Zephyr became the ticket office and waiting area for Amtrak passengers. When Amtrak later built their new facility, the California Zephyr was retired. It now houses the Maricopa Historical Society Museum.

It's clear that all of our carefully laid plans and worthy designs added value by making good things even better. Adding value takes creativity!

# CHAPTER ELEVEN
# THE POWER OF CREATIVE MARKETING

You've probably figured out by now that Zig Ziglar was a long-time close friend of mine, as well as a confidante and a trusted mentor. I will always be proud to have known him and his wife, Jean, whom he affectionately called "The Redhead." I worked closely with him for many years. In fact, it was Zig who introduced me to the Horatio Alger Award, of which he was a great admirer. The prestigious award is given to outstanding Americans who, through determination and hard work, have risen from abject poverty to become successes in their fields of endeavor and have spread that success to others.

Zig always loved my stories about marketing, and he suggested I write a book about creative marketing. That was my original intent when I started working on this book, but I soon realized there were many additional principles I've tried to apply in both my business and personal life. That's how this book became *Success Demands a Master Plan*. In Zig's honor, I'm now going to give special attention to the principles of creative marketing because it has been an essential element of my success.

The first thing I learned about creative marketing was this:

> *Find a way to give your customers something of real value and they'll want more of it.*

## 11. The Power of Creative Marketing

Zig Ziglar, his wife "The Redhead" Jean, Sheila and me.

### Ten-by-Ten

I trace my marketing philosophy back to my early working days. After graduating from college, I accepted a position with American Stores Packing Company. I was there for only two years, and working in a meat packing plant definitely wasn't my passion, but I learned a great deal. It was while working for American Stores that I picked up an evening and weekend sales position with Kirby vacuum cleaners—yes, doing those in-home demonstrations. Kirby was and is a great company because they really make a great product.

## 11. The Power of Creative Marketing

Kirby had two offers to entice potential customers to invite us into their homes. *Free Offer A* was a set of steak knives, which often turned into, "Show me your vacuum cleaner, then give me my knives and leave." *Free Offer B* involved the salesperson shampooing a ten-by-ten foot area of the prospect's carpeting to demonstrate the power and efficiency of the Kirby system.

My Kirby office would obtain leads and turn those leads over to a team of salespeople. Most of the sales staff were older than I was, and they'd been selling Kirby products for years. They wanted the easy sales. They would scour the leads and choose those customers who wanted *Free Offer A*. By the time I arrived at the office after my day job, I was pleased to discover that the experienced salespeople had passed over the prospects who had chosen *Free Offer B*—the ten-by-ten foot area carpet shampoo. They preferred to deliver knives rather than work harder and shampoo a carpet.

Armed with the best equipment money could buy, I would knock on doors and announce, "I'm here to clean a ten-by-ten foot area of your carpet. Where would you like me to do this?" Invariably, the prospect would lead me into a room that was twelve-by-sixteen or sixteen-by-twenty. There seemed to be few rooms that were actually ten-by-ten.

I'd mark out a ten-by-ten foot area, vacuum it thoroughly, then shampoo it as they watched intently. The results were amazing! Carpet that was having a near-death experience would come back to life! "What do you think?" I'd ask.

"Amazing," they'd reply. "But . . . um . . . now only that little ten-by-ten foot area is clean. What about the rest of it?"

## 11. The Power of Creative Marketing

Bingo—another sale! I quickly became Kirby's number one salesperson in the area because I took on the prospects that involved actual work, and because I learned that if I gave customers something good, they would want more of it.

I admit there were more than a few times when an elderly prospect couldn't afford a shiny new Kirby with all the attachments. In those cases, I would either stay behind and finish shampooing the carpet or, if I had another appointment, volunteer to come back. Two reputations were on the line—Kirby's and mine. Stranding people isn't the way to build a good reputation.

The second thing I learned about creative marketing is:
*If you have a quality product, creative marketing can help you introduce it to new markets.*

### Spot On!

One of my good friends is a man named Barry Meguiar. You may know him as the gregarious host of the television show *Car Crazy*, where he traveled the world interviewing car enthusiasts. Back in the early 1900s, Barry's grandfather had started a company called Meguiar's Wax. He sold a high-quality wax used by furniture manufacturers to protect their lacquered furniture. That was its only market.

A few years later, the automobile industry was born, and cars were painted with lacquer. Grandpa Meguiar began to sell his product to Ford Motor Company and other early car builders. After opening up the automobile market for furniture wax, Meguiar began selling its wax to automotive body shops. But still, all sales were to professionals within the industry.

Then Barry got involved in the family business in sales.

## 11. The Power of Creative Marketing

An admitted *car guy*, he loves the sculptured look, the smell, the sound, and the power of a beautiful automobile. He's one of those guys the Beach Boys wrote their hit songs about; songs, like "409" and "Little Deuce Coupe."

Several years ago, Barry got hooked on exotic car auctions, such as the famous Barrett-Jackson shows that occurred all over the country. Barry also had the creative marketing gene. One fine day, he went to a show and took several cans of Meguiar's wax with him. He asked the owner of an expensive car that was being prepped for auction if he could demonstrate his wax. The owner said yes, so Barry waxed an area about a foot in diameter. Then he asked, "What do you think?"

The owner said, "Wow! But now the rest of the car looks dull. What am I supposed to do about that?"

Barry replied, "Tell you what. I'll give you the remaining wax so you can finish polishing your car. But I'd like you to put a sign in your window that reads, 'Shine by Meguiar's Wax.'"

Barry then moved on to the next car in the show area, then the next, and the next. By the time he'd finished his rounds, nearly every car on the lot had Meguiar's wax on the body and a Meguiar's sign in the window. A huge new market was born. Today, Barry's products are arguably the most respected in the industry. I call his innovative technique "Spot On Marketing."

I'm sure you've noticed that both of these stories have three things in common:
1. A convincing demonstration of a quality product.
2. The customer's desire for more.
3. A readily available solution, offered without delay.

## 11. The Power of Creative Marketing

You may be thinking now, "Wait a minute. You both blackmailed your prospects. You shampooed a ten-by-ten foot area, and Barry waxed a tiny spot on a big car."

I believe the difference between creative marketing and blackmail is clear: Creative marketing arrives at one's door, dressed as "ethics" and "integrity." A true creative marketer:

- Never strands the customer in an uncomfortable position.
- Always identifies a customer's true needs and wants.
- Always leaves a satisfied customer behind.

Yes, I shampooed a ten-by-ten-foot area. But even if the customer couldn't afford to buy a Kirby—or didn't want to buy one—I finished the job. Yes, Barry waxed a small section of a show car after getting the owner's permission to do so. But he also gave the owner free wax. Don't you see that every aspect of each arrangement was based on a fair trade? I do.

In each case, customers' needs and wants were identified. In the first case, my prospects desired a clean home. In Barry's case, a shiny, sparkling car was in a better position to draw top dollar in an auction. In both cases, customers were satisfied, either by service or quality or both.

Here, then, is the third principle of creative marketing and the third story in this chapter:

*Identify what the customer really wants or needs*
*and deliver it in unforgettable ways.*

## 11. The Power of Creative Marketing

### Rat Bait

I've told you about my years with Tufts & Son of Oklahoma. In many respects, John Tufts, Sr. was as much a father to me as Virgil Haley, who was a powerful influence in my life after my father died. John gave me the opportunity to be the sales force for our new company in the state of Oklahoma. It seemed like a dream career. I owned fifty percent of my future!

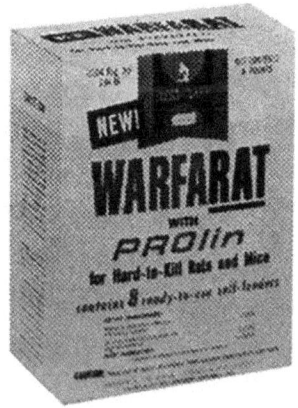

**The product that gave me the reputation as the "Number One Rat Bait Salesperson in America".**

One of the wisest men I've ever met, John, told me, "The people who can do it can't tell you how to do it. Those who can tell you how to do it can't do it." I think he misjudged himself, though. He could both do it and tell me how to do it.

Our company sold animal health-related products and vet medicine to farm stores, feed stores, veterinarians, and co-ops. We would buy from manufacturers and sell to the retail outlets. They, in turn, would sell the products to farmers and ranchers.

## 11. The Power of Creative Marketing

One of the ongoing problems farmers and ranchers faced was that of controlling pests. And among the major pests they had to deal with were rats and mice—ugly, dirty, destructive, contaminated rodents. To control them, they relied on rat bait. You've likely heard of d-CON. It's the standard rat bait containing Warfarin. Along came a brand new rat bait with the exact chemical found in d-CON. It was manufactured by Hess & Clark, who happened to own the patent to Warfarin. We had a lot of competitors in the field, and many of them also sold Hess & Clark products.

Hess & Clark made an introductory offer to us we could offer to our customers: "If you buy two cases, you get one case free." The basic idea was to encourage salespeople to offer a discount to customers, which they did. We knew our competitors would pounce on our existing customers with this offer to try to win their other business away from us as well.

I spent some time thinking about ways to set ourselves apart from our competition. The manufacturer offered two different package sizes. They had a three-pound bulk pack containing "throw packs" that sold to the dealers wholesale for twelve dollars a case, and they had a one-pound size packaged twenty to a case that sold for twenty dollars a case. My question to the manufacturer was, "If I buy two cases of the three-pound size, which had a dealer cost of twelve dollars each, can I take my free goods in the more expensive, one-pound, twenty-dollar case size?"

They informed me, "No, you'll have to take your free goods in the same size that you buy the first two."

Then I asked, "What if I buy 500 cases?"

## 11. The Power of Creative Marketing

The salesman checked with his sales manager in Ohio, and it was decided if I bought 500 cases, they'd let me take my free goods however I wanted them. For every two cases of the throw packs, which sold to the dealer for twelve dollars each, I took my free goods in the one-pound size that I sold to the dealer for twenty dollars each.

Here's where creative marketing comes into play. Instead of giving them free product with each purchase, as my competition was doing, I offered something completely different, something really exciting! I went to Winchester Repeating Arms, the gun manufacturer, and told them I wanted to buy Winchester Model 190, .22 caliber, semi-automatic rifles and give them away as a premium gift. These rifles sold for between eighty-eight- and ninety-two-dollars retail, depending on whether they were on special. Winchester agreed to let us buy them in lots of one hundred. They would ship them to me through their distributor at the cost of thirty dollars per rifle. Now I had a way to drive the rat bait business!

I'd walk into the dealer carrying packages of Hess & Clark's new rat bait, Warfarin, in one hand, and a brand-new Winchester .22 rifle under the other arm and present my card—Tufts & Son of Oklahoma. If you know anything about rural America, you know rifles are a really big deal. It doesn't matter if you already own a semi-automatic .22 rifle, you'd always like one more.

It was something to see! Dealers would leave paying customers standing at the cash register and come over to check what I had. The same dealers who hadn't given me the time of day on the last call asked, "What's the deal with the rifle?"

## 11. The Power of Creative Marketing

I'd answer, "I've got a promotion you're going to remember. Whether you buy it or not, I guarantee you'll remember it."

"OK, let's see it!" they'd say.

I'd explain, "Hess & Clark has a brand-new rat bait that contains Warfarin, just like the product you have on your shelf. I want you to buy four cases of these new little throw packs of rat bait. Your cost is twelve dollars a case. That's four times twelve dollars or forty-eight dollars' worth of rat bait. I also want you to buy two cases of the one-pound size. Those two cases will cost you two times twenty dollars or forty dollars. Your total cost is eighty-eight dollars. Now, when you buy this, you're going to receive a Winchester 190, .22 semi-automatic rifle with a four-power scope absolutely free, along with your six cases of the best rat bait made." The free goods that I sold more than paid for the thirty-dollar rifles.

They'd look at me, look at my card, look at me again and say, "Son, I'm going to try you just this one time. This deal better be just like you said it was, or I'm going to get a gun and I'm going to find you."

I heard that over and over again. Yet, they bought every time because I was giving them a ninety-dollar rifle with an eighty-eight-dollar purchase of rat bait. Remember, this rifle only cost me thirty dollars. I bought it with the forty dollars they paid me for my free goods, leaving a ten-dollar extra profit per deal for me. On top of that, I was also making my regular profit on my four cases of throw packs. It was a very profitable transaction for me. And I never made a presentation—ever—where I didn't sell a rat bait deal.

## 11. The Power of Creative Marketing

Sometimes, customers would ask, "Are you sure this rat bait's any good?" Then they'd think for a minute and say, "Aw, well, never mind. If it isn't, I've got a rifle, and I'll shoot them."

During this time, two of the best peddlers this world has ever known joined me. Ed Jessup and Sam Holman became part of a very successful team that eventually grew to six salespeople strong in Oklahoma alone. We were shipping out rifles left and right, and we made sure the customers got them even before the rat bait came in. Soon we were on our third railcar load of rat bait. We delivered more than 500 rifles and were attracting new customers daily.

One day I was getting ready to go on a sales call when I saw a black car pull up in front of our office. Two guys in suits stepped out of the car. Sheila came into my office and said, "There are two men out there with badges, and they'd like to talk to you."

They came into my office and showed me their credentials. They were with the Department of Alcohol, Tobacco, and Firearms and were "visiting" from Dallas, Texas. They wanted to know what my intent was with the 500 rifles I'd purchased. By then, I was on my third carload of rat bait.

I asked them to sit down, pulled out my detail book, and showed them the rat bait deal. I went through all the details of the transaction with them. They looked at each other. Then one of them turned to me and asked, "Could we buy a rat bait deal?"

I replied, "No, you can't buy a rat bait deal—we sell strictly to wholesale customers with sales tax numbers. But I can give you a copy of our sales flier for your records."

## 11. The Power of Creative Marketing

"That would help," they said. "The guys back in the office will never believe this story."

After I gave them a copy of the deal, I said, "I'll do one more thing for you." Throughout the promotion, I'd asked Sheila to keep a list of names and driver's license numbers of everyone who received a gun, just in case the question ever came up. I asked, "Would you like that list?"

They said, "Yes," so I gave it to them. Then they got up and went out the door laughing all the way, got in their car, and drove back to Dallas.

I need to say a special thank you to Rod Reinke, the Hess & Clark rep, for helping make me the "Number One Rat Bait Salesman in America," as proclaimed by Zig Ziglar.

That's not my only example of creative marketing.

## Booting Up

After that promotion wound down, I decided to try something new and connected with Tony Lama, Jr., the famous bootmaker. I wanted to offer his cowboy boots. In the West, boots are like .22 rifles; you can always use at least one more pair. If you wear boots, you know you can't have too many.

Their sales rep was Lynn Laske. I told him how successful I'd been with the rifles, but Tony Lama still didn't want to cut me a deal with boots because he didn't want me competing with Sheplers, one of their major retail customers. I told him, "I will never *sell* your boots to anyone. If you ever have one complaint from Sheplers, I will understand and the deal's off."

After much persuading by Lynn, Tony agreed to set me

up, and I was able to buy cowhide boots worth one hundred dollars for only thirty dollars. I also bought some lizard and ostrich boots at well below their retail price.

For this promotion, I put together a deal with Pfizer that was similar to the rat bait offer. Every fall, Pfizer came out with a special on Terramycin 500-milliliter bottles. It's liquid, injectable oxytetracycline, the standard in the veterinary industry. Pfizer was offering a ten percent fall promotion discount, and my competition was selling five-case deals that cost the dealer $500 or $100 per case. They were offering the dealer a ten percent or $50 discount.

Instead of giving the dealers a $50 discount, I showed them a Tony Lama catalog. I was selling the same product as my competition, but I offered them a $100 pair of boots for a $500 order. Meanwhile, I was paying only $30 for the boots. Of course, the dealers looked at the catalog and decided they wanted a $100 pair of boots instead of a $50 discount. I made an extra $20 on the deal.

They also had to decide if they wanted five cases, ten, or twenty cases because if their business justified it, they could get a pair of lizard boots with a ten-case order, or they could get a pair of ostrich boots with a twenty-case order.

I was giving away boots left and right, of course. We were using creative marketing to differentiate ourselves from our competitors and make a higher profit at the same time.

## CB Radios and Stetson Hats

Following that promotion, I made a very similar offer with a product from Cobra—CB radios. Before cell phones, CB radios were very popular. Every person you

## 11. The Power of Creative Marketing

met—husband, wife, and kid—had a CB radio in their vehicle. Cobra was the top of the line.

From there I went to Stetson hats . . . and the list goes on and on.

### The "Perfect" Promotion

During this time, I discovered that the National Finals Rodeo was a very hot ticket item in Oklahoma. I'd been asked to help promote the event, so I challenged myself to come up with something "out of the box" again. I'd just built a new warehouse in Oklahoma City for our ever-expanding company and was planning an open house. So, I bought 1,100 tickets and decided to put on a trade show. The idea was to invite all our manufacturers to set up booths to display their products. I sold display space to about 300 manufacturers who'd come to show their products. Then I invited my customers to come in and meet with the manufacturers and receive some great discounts. Not only did they get discounts, but they also got great entertainment. On Friday night before the rodeo started, I brought in c stars directly from Nashville and threw a big barbecue. Then I took our top 1,100 customers to the rodeo, which became the hottest ticket in the country. The trade show was such a huge success, I made it an annual event and called it the Tufts & Son Annual Trade Show. We were writing millions of dollars of business in a two-day period—Friday and Saturday—during the first part of each December. Our trade show eventually became the standard in the nation.

As I traveled calling on my customers, I might find a shipment from my competitor. The customers would be embarrassed and start making excuses about why they had purchased it. I would kid them and say, "Bring your binoculars to the rodeo next year because your seats will be way up top." We would all laugh, but they got the message. I've shown again and again that creative marketing can give every business an unbeatable edge! And I'm not the only one to prove it. Hal Morris is a perfect example.

## Hal Morris and the Airplane to Nowhere

Many of my friends today are men I met as a youth. Each summer, I earned my way to summer camp in New Mexico. It was at camp that I met a young Hal Morris, who later became a close friend during my freshman year at college.

Hal didn't come from a family with money, so he knew he'd have to be creative to pay for his education. And was he creative! He'd drive down to Mexico and purchase paintings that were done on black velvet. You've seen them—Elvis Presley is a popular subject. He convinced a store owner near the college to take the paintings on consignment. Then he'd split the profits with the store. This worked well for Hal, despite all the ridicule the other students heaped on him.

But conventional college studies didn't appeal to Hal. Instead, he found he had a natural aptitude for real estate and the stock market. He studied hard, then applied for and got a job with Paine, Webber, Jackson & Curtis, now UBS AG. One of his first moves was to ask for the names of the ten most successful brokers. Then he called them and secured interviews with four of the top ten.

One of the four, a young broker from California, shared a secret with him. "Fake it until you make it," he said. He

## 11. The Power of Creative Marketing

explained to Hal that when the markets closed at 1:00 p.m., he would hustle over to the Santa Anita, Hollywood Park, or Del Mar racetracks, still in his three-piece suit. He'd sit in his box seat and place tiny bets in the Jockey Club. The wealthier race fans placed much larger bets, but they never knew the tiny amount the young broker was betting. They noticed him and asked what he did for a living. "I'm a stockbroker," he replied.

"Well, you must be really successful if you can be at the race track every day," they observed. Slowly but surely, the people who frequented the track became his customers, and he was enormously successful.

Hal took his cue from this lesson. He decided to offer free investment seminars in smaller towns that were not served by investment counselors or brokerage houses. One such town within easy traveling distance was Lake Havasu, Arizona, on the California/Arizona border. Hal knew from his research that quite a few wealthy people had retired there. He took out an ad in the local paper that said, "Hal Morris will be flying into Lake Havasu this Wednesday for a FREE Investment Seminar at the Holiday Inn."

The fact that someone would charter a plane and fly into their little town to offer a free seminar intrigued the locals, so they checked it out. Hal would pick four stocks during each visit and ask the attendees to track them and report back the next time he flew in. He'd do his research, often talking to the presidents of the companies whose stocks he'd picked, and sure enough, those stocks would go up. This impressed the residents of Lake Havasu, and many became his loyal customers. Hal built a successful career by applying the three principles of creative marketing.

## 11. The Power of Creative Marketing

1. He found a way to give his customers *something of real value,* so they wanted more.
2. He had a *quality product,* and creative marketing helped him introduce it to new markets.
3. He *identified what the customer wanted or needed and then delivered it in an unforgettable way.*

As a result of his success, Hal Morris has appeared on major cable network financial programs—including MSNBC, CNN, and others—and the *Wall Street Journal* once referred to him as the "Wunderkind of Wall Street."

I've long been inspired by people like Barry Meguiar and Hal Morris. They demonstrate that success is within reach of all of us, no matter our upbringing, education, or passions.

A final word: There are always ways to separate yourself from the crowd. Get creative and differentiate yourself and your company. If you're not constantly seeking ways to stand out through creative marketing, you're missing out on enormous opportunities.

## CHAPTER TWELVE
# THE POWER OF SERVICE

The plain truth in business is that if you don't serve your customers well, you won't have any customers. As a result of many years of personal experience, here are my keys to powerful service: I call them the "FOUR C's."

1. Creativity
2. Consistency
3. Commitment
4. Continuity

## Creativity

By creativity, I mean doing things a little differently in order to stand out from the pack. Years ago, I thought that Burger King had the greatest concept ever. They were going up against McDonald's with a simple idea that they highlighted in a clever jingle in their TV commercials. Do you remember this?

*"Hold the pickle, hold the lettuce*
*Special orders don't upset us*
*All we ask is that you let us serve it your way"*

*"Your way."* What a great concept! Who doesn't want it *their* way? What customer ever said "Thank you for your offer to let me have it *my* way, but I prefer to have it

## 12. The Power of Service

*your* way. And I'd like to pay more for it too." And that's how creativity became an essential part of Burger King's customer service program.

There are other ways of being creative. It may mean delivering the product in a creative way, like creative packaging. I don't know about you, but I prefer my soft drinks to have some fizz when I drink them. In the old days, when Coke or Pepsi came in a can, the fizz started to dissipate when I removed the top or popped the tab. There was no way to replace the cap or the pull-tab. Then someone invented screw-top plastic bottles. Now I can hit the road with a fresh soda, reseal it from time to time, and still enjoy some fizz an hour later. Packaging, in this and many other ways, has evolved.

What about a creative delivery system? Every time you stop at the drive-through windows at McDonald's, Arby's, Burger King, Starbucks, or even a drugstore, you're experiencing it. Fast is good, right?

The key here is that you always must be programmed to sell, and in the way you want to sell, the way that makes you most comfortable and successful. For McDonald's, it's the drive-through windows, the simplified menu selection, and the quick ordering and delivery. For you, it may be other things. You always need to ask, "What will make it the easiest for people to buy my product?"

## Consistency

What most people don't realize, whether they're employers or team members, is that it's not always the big things that make a difference in the minds of customers.

## 12. The Power of Service

More often than not, it's the little things that make people and organizations stand out. It's the smiles, the handshakes, the words of appreciation, and the genuine "thank you" that customers remember.

In the early years of my business, Sheila was the best there was at this. There wasn't a package or invoice going out that didn't include a personal note of appreciation from her. She simply wrote on the packing slip; other times she wrote a special note and included it in the shipment. She also had an uncanny ability to recognize the telephone voices of our customers before they even identified themselves. This was long before Caller ID. And we had over 1,000 customers. She always managed to make every customer feel special.

Customers notice when the little things change. No matter what service standard you set, make sure it's consistent and ongoing. The tiniest change can diminish customer loyalty. Have you ever returned to your favorite place—a store, restaurant, national park, campground, or hotel—and discovered something you loved had changed? Your favorite trail is no longer open at your favorite campground, no fitness center at your favorite hotel—it's now a bar instead.

While I don't advocate preserving unprofitable aspects of any venture, the consistency of what you offer and the customer service offered with it are vital to your ongoing success. Think about Burger King again. Years ago, they announced they were dropping the "Whopper," and customers were so upset, the company brought back this overwhelmingly popular item. Or consider Coca-Cola. When they introduced "New Coke" and dropped the old formula, loyalists went crazy. So they reintroduced the old formula and called it "Coca-Cola Classic." These incidents demonstrate the customers' desire for consistency.

## Commitment

There are three elements of commitment involved in effective customer service. These are:

1. Commitment to training the team.
2. Commitment to customer satisfaction.
3. Commitment to offering a quality product or service.

A poorly trained team—a team made up of people who don't fully realize the importance of their roles—is a formula for failure. *Training the team* simply means telling every individual *why* they're on the team, *what* they're expected to do, *how* they're expected to do it, and *when* they're expected to do it. These are issues like timeliness, deadlines, and expectations. I can't say it often enough. In all four key points, specifics are important. There's no room for vagueness. Training really is as simple as that.

*Customer satisfaction* means that every member of the team does whatever is necessary to make the customer want to be a returning customer. It's what Ken Blanchard and Sheldon Bowles refer to as creating "Raving Fans" in their book of that title. It's amazing how little it takes to turn a customer into a former customer. Imagine if my investors never made money on any of their investments in El Dorado Holdings. Not only would I never see them again, but I'm sure they'd tell everyone they knew they were dissatisfied.

## 12. The Power of Service

Finally, offering *a quality product or service* is paramount. But please remember that even if your product or service is top-notch, you have to back it up with a competent team and a commitment to customer satisfaction.

## Continuity

Continuity means follow-through. It's a simple principle. If you promise something, you do it. If the message on your voicemail says, "Your call is important to us—leave a message and we'll call back," you call back. If you promise delivery on a certain day by a certain time, you deliver. If you offer a guarantee on your product or service, you meet that obligation. This is what continuity really is.

There are two key words in the term "Customer Service." The first word is "customer." It's the reason you're in business. Your customer is the one whose loyalty and positive word of mouth keeps you in business. The second word is "service." It's your key to earning that loyalty and fostering positive feelings from your customers.

While building my distribution business in Oklahoma, there were two things that set me apart from my competition:

1. We always answered the phone by its second ring and never put someone on hold without their permission. Then we checked back every thirty seconds.
2. When we left in the evening, which was usually after 6:00 p.m., phone calls were forwarded to my home. My customers could reach me twenty-four hours a day. Many times, I would get a call during the night from a veterinarian needing something immediately.

## 12. The Power of Service

If there wasn't a bus going that way, I would drive it to them myself.

An effective Master Plan for any business involves building a customer base, then giving those customers the continuous level of service that will make them long-term customers.

## CHAPTER THIRTEEN
# THE POWER OF THINKING BIG

### "Think Big!"

I believe these words should apply to every area of life. People who think small, have small ideas, set small goals, and follow small dreams will never achieve big things. President John F. Kennedy once said, "Those who dare to fail miserably can achieve greatly." He's suggesting we think big, that we dare to take on bold challenges, realizing that we can fail. My belief is that failing to dream big dreams is the biggest failure of all.

The key to "bigness" is the power of scalability, the ability of a business to grow larger. If you have a sound idea backed with a workable plan, there's no reason why you can't take that idea to the next level. And the next. And the next after that.

### Chick-fil-A

Think about a company like Chick-fil-A. It's successful in the field of quick-service restaurants. (Sounds better than fast food, doesn't it?) I'm using Chick-fil-A as an example, because I have a deep appreciation for their values. Their corporate culture rewards employee loyalty and puts faith and family first. They've provided millions of dollars in scholarships to young college students, and they're closed on Sundays so that families can play, worship, and celebrate life together.

## 13. The Power of Thinking Big

Their founder, the late S. Truett Cathy—a man who long held to the importance of all these values—started with one restaurant back in 1946. His first restaurant, The Dwarf House, was across the street from a Ford Motor Company assembly plant in Hapeville, Georgia.

In the early 1960s, he invented the boneless chicken breast sandwich and founded Chick-fil-A, Inc. In 1967, he pioneered the establishment of his restaurants in shopping malls with the opening of his first Chick-fil-A at a mall in suburban Atlanta. Since then, Chick-fil-A has grown to become the third-largest, quick-service restaurant chain in the United States, with more than 3,279 locations in forty-eight states and Washington, D.C. In 2019, after fifty consecutive years of sales growth, the chain reported more than $22.7 billion in revenue.

Yes, there are larger chains of fast-food restaurants, like McDonalds and Starbucks. But all three of these chains are perfect examples of thinking big. With scalability, there's always room to grow.

### Carpet Cleaning

Thinking big doesn't apply just to restaurants. My good friend, Wes Bates, is in an entirely different industry. His company cleans carpets. When Wes graduated from college, he had no idea what he really wanted to do. So, he went to work for his father, Jack, who owned a small carpet-cleaning company in Columbus, Ohio. Wes likes to joke that he was the most highly educated carpet cleaner in Ohio.

Since he was technically minded, Wes determined there could be a better way to clean carpets. He designed and

## 13. The Power of Thinking Big

built a 260-pound carpet-cleaning machine on wheels. It could be rolled off a truck and into a home, and the sixteen feet of hose attached could reach every corner of most houses. When operated by someone who knew the basics of cleaning carpets, it worked wonders.

With the first two machines out in the field, Wes and his dad realized there would be a market for this device. They built more of them, and Wes went out on the road to sell them to others in the carpet-cleaning business. Back in 1972, the price of the unit was $4,295. Wes earned a thousand dollars for each machine he sold.

Most weeks, he sold one or two. But the machine caught on, and one week, he sold four. That meant $4,000 in commissions. His dad said, "No way am I paying you that much money." Wes thought to himself, "Why am I breaking my back out on the road to sell these things, if I'm not going to be paid?" Still, he knew they'd created a virtually indestructible machine that could have a growing market. Wes needed to get his dad to think big and convinced him to form a joint venture and offer franchises.

Wes ran an ad in the Columbus newspaper offering opportunities in Florida. The headline read, "Do we have a deal for you in Florida!" People eager to escape Ohio winters responded, and the truck-mounted machines began to move out the door on the road to Florida. Jack wanted to call the growing company "Jack Rabbit Carpet Cleaning," but they ultimately settled on "Stanley Steemer."

I'm guessing you've heard of Stanley Steemer. They're a highly respected name in the industry. They have 350 offices around the country in 49 states, 329 individual franchisees,

## 13. The Power of Thinking Big

a fleet of 1,000 trucks, and 2,500 employees. They spend $50 million in television advertising every year, and they've used the internet to make online booking of their services easy, fast, and dependable.

Stanley Steemer's business plan is simple: Stick with the core business, don't get sidetracked, treat people well—especially customers—and make the people around you successful. In addition, reinvest in the company rather than buying a Rolls-Royce and living the grand life.

In short, Stanley Steemer has become a scalable company. They've attracted the attention of several larger companies that want to buy them out, but they've adhered to their principles, defended their franchisees, and refused extremely lucrative offers.

In order to expand their business, in 1998, they added another service to clean the air conditioning and heating ducts in the homes. People could rid their ducts of the dirt, dust and microbial growth that naturally occur over the years, causing allergy issues and other health problems. Along with this innovation, they also created a system known as Restore. Restore contains two essential components that make it so powerful: a positively charged carbon matrix that captures compounds that enter the system and an ultraviolet light that sterilizes the compounds. This service is now available in forty-nine states throughout the nation. During the COVID-19 epidemic in 2020, this service grew exponentially, as thousands of households sought to obtain the cleanest environment possible. I offer this service to our employees. Yes, I want healthy employees and their families.

### 13. The Power of Thinking Big

I believe it provides a service for both the employees and me with less sick days and a healthier environment at the office.

The 2000s led to additional Stanley Steemer services, including tile and grout cleaning, hardwood floor cleaning, and off-site oriental and fine area-rug cleaning.

**Catch of the Day with Wes Bates at Johnny Morris' Calhoun Pits.**

By now, you must be asking, "How do companies—and ideas—become scalable?" It simply means:
- Have a good idea.
- Have an idea that has wide appeal.
- Have an idea that can be profitable.
- Have an idea that can be replicated.

## 13. The Power of Thinking Big

This model has worked for Chick-fil-A and Stanley Steemer. It's also worked for such diverse concepts as Victoria's Secret, Red Lobster, Olive Garden, and Chico's, the women's fashion store.

### Richard J. Stephenson

Richard J. Stephenson is a highly successful international merchant banker, entrepreneur, and philanthropist. He graduated in 1962 from Wabash College and, while earning his J.D. degree from Northwestern University, established International Capital Investment Company (ICIC) where he still serves as chairman. He was also the founder and chairman of Cancer Treatment Centers of America (CTCA®) since the company's inception in 1988. Richard sold that enterprise to City of Hope in 2022 but remains as chairman. He is an example of someone who "thought big" to meet significant needs! Richard was taught by his parents to live a life in accordance with this moral code: "When you see someone who is less well off than yourself and you're in a unique position to do something about their plight—without harm to self, family or Lord—you simply step into the opportunity and do it." No fuss, no muss, no conversation. Just do it!

Following his mother's death from cancer—and the painful reality of her lack of hope-fulfilling options, treatment and care—my friend made a promise to change the face of cancer care: "I never wanted to see another cancer patient suffer the agony of living without hope." Thus, he and his family founded CTCA® to fulfill that promise, and they introduced to the world what he aptly coined the "Mother

## 13. The Power of Thinking Big

Standard" of care, the kind of care you would want for your own loved one.

During Richard's tenure as chairman, CTCA® pioneered and proved the importance of a new paradigm in cancer care that empowers patients and their caregivers by providing them with services and programs they desire, where and when they desire them, in one seamless and comprehensive setting. As a result, they are offered more innovative, integrated, and hopeful options with which to better manage their cancer and enjoy a greatly enhanced quality of life.

Today, through its national network of hospitals specializing in the treatment of adult patients with cancer, CTCA® offers an integrated approach to care that combines advancements in precision cancer treatment, surgery, radiation, chemotherapy, and immunotherapy—with supportive therapies designed to manage side effects and enhance quality of life both during and after treatment. The network also offers a range of clinical trials to reveal new treatment options supported by scientific and investigational research. It's rated in national consumer surveys as one of the most admired hospital systems in the U.S. Now, as part of the ever-growing City of Hope, CTCA® is recognized as a national leader in cancer treatment and one of the nation's top five hospitals for cancer care, according to *U.S. News & World Report's* 2024–25 ranking.

In 1991, Richard also founded Gateway for Cancer Research, which he still chairs and supports. To date they have raised over $75 million to fund more than 140 cutting-edge clinical trials around the world. This nonprofit organization spends ninety-nine cents of every dollar

## 13. The Power of Thinking Big

received from public contributions to fund these trials that have brought hope to thousands of cancer patients.

Today, the Stephenson family, including Richard's wife, Dr. Stacie Stephenson and their five children, are all actively and passionately devoted to this mission.

### El Dorado Holdings (Cortaro Ranch)

In my business of real estate development, the same principles apply. Here's how it worked in the development of the city of Maricopa:

- Develop land by adding value. (A good idea)
- Offer a community that is affordable. (Wide appeal)
- Make a reasonable return on investment. (Be profitable)
- Create other neighborhoods/communities that follow a similar plan. (Replication)

We've successfully used the power of "Thinking Big" by replicating our project in Maricopa. We've added other neighborhoods modeled after the first one, such as in Queen Creek, a suburb of Phoenix, and Tucson, a city approximately a hundred miles southeast of Phoenix.

The Tucson development, known as Cortaro Ranch, also required some creative thinking on our part. Norm McClelland of Shamrock Farms and his family had owned the land in Marana, north of Tucson, for more than five decades. Unfortunately for any potential developer, Norm had made the mistake of clearing the dairy cattle off the land several years before he called me to ask if I was interested. If he'd continued to use the land to raise milking cattle, I could

## 13. The Power of Thinking Big

have easily convinced the neighbors to support anything else because they would have gotten rid of the smell, the flies, the odor, and the nuisance of having a dairy farm in their backyard.

But he took care of that problem himself, removed the nuisance, and since that time, the neighbors had decided that this was their place to ride horses and dirt bikes. It was their place to go walking. It was their personal recreational park. Although it was private property, in their minds, they'd laid claim to it. This made it difficult to get the neighbors to support anything we'd hoped to do in terms of zoning. They felt we were taking away an amenity that fell into their laps.

On top of that obstacle, I soon discovered that underneath this property lay one of the largest known Native American archaeological finds in the state of Arizona. The University of Arizona had already dubbed the land as "The Dairy Site" because of the dairy farm that had been there for years. To develop this piece of property, I had to gain the support of the major conservancy groups, the archaeological groups, a Native American tribe, and the neighbors who rode their horses on it.

The Tohono O'odham Nation had to be convinced that our potential development would benefit them somehow. I'd discovered from developing the road to Maricopa and working with the Ak-Chin and the Gila River communities that Native American leaders are open-minded to new ideas. But like any group I've negotiated with, they have to know what's in it for them and their people.

Their primary concern was that we would maintain their sacred grounds and not desecrate them in any way. So,

## 13. The Power of Thinking Big

in developing this property, I agreed that any time we were removing dirt in excess of six inches at a time, or making a cut in the soil, I would have a Tohono O'odham representative on the site to inspect. As we started this process, we uncovered wonderful fire pits and ancient gathering places, as well as houses where the previous inhabitants had lived, along with evidence of how they lived. We were excited and so was the University of Arizona archaeological department.

It was all buried under three to six feet of dust that had been windblown for centuries. Our plan involved setting aside some archaeological property that would never be disturbed. It was fenced off and secured in such a way that it would be preserved for all time. We recovered and paid for a lot of archaeological finds, as well as for their preservation. It took several years of negotiations to make certain that the tribe was satisfied with how things would be handled and that the city council and mayor would be happy.

The biggest problem, though, was appeasing the neighbors who had come to know and use this private area as a public recreational facility. The solution was to set aside additional community property and create parks and riding trails for the existing neighbors, as well as for the new residents.

Over time, it all came together because of these principles of "Thinking Big":

- Developing land by adding value was a good idea.
- Offering home sites in a community that was affordable had wide appeal.
- Giving our investors a reasonable return on their investment made it profitable.

- Replicating by creating other communities that follow a similar Master Plan was a good and profitable idea.

## El Dorado Holdings (Douglas Ranch)

The same principles of "Thinking Big" came into play in another large property holding we went in on around 2005 with JDM Partners LLC, headed by Jerry Colangelo, David Eaton, and Mel Schultz. It was approximately 37,000 acres (or about fifty-three square miles) of beautiful, undeveloped desert land, backing up to the White Tank Mountains and known as Douglas Ranch. We planned to make Douglas Ranch a reality by developing land through adding value, by offering a community that was affordable, and making a reasonable, but not excessive, return on our investment.

Our plan was to make Douglas Ranch a "smart city," keeping it as environmentally "clean" as possible. It would be directly on the corridor of the new Interstate 11, which would link Phoenix and Las Vegas—the first Interstate Highway to do that. Thanks to the involvement of Mary Peters, the Secretary of Transportation under President George W. Bush, $100 million in land value was ready for donation, targeted and proposed for the future right-of-way.

We had a 50/50 ownership with JDM Partners. We worked hard on our investment, putting together the plan, the entitlements, everything that was needed, and had it in escrow in 2007. As I mentioned earlier, 2007 was when the crash came, the last recession, which lasted until 2009. We had a New York City real estate group interested in buying one-third interest as a silent partner and more than doubled their investment. We would have made money for our

## 13. The Power of Thinking Big

investors and still developed the property. Two years went by, and we came close, but the deal never closed. When everything crashed, everything crashed.

Here's something I learned in all my years in real estate. When things are good, you think they're going to be good forever; when things are bad, you think they're going to be bad forever. But neither is true. There's always going to be a correction that will level things out. Then you'll be back to another cycle. It's just not always pleasant getting there. So, we kept preparing the land and moving forward with what would become Interstate 11, knowing how badly Phoenix needed new housing for all the people who were moving there.

Then, in 2021, when Douglas Ranch was in the late planning stages, the Howard Hughes Corporation (HHC) made an offer to purchase the property for $600 million. We were able to pay back our patient investors (who'd been waiting for sixteen years) and had enough money to make another investment in Florence, Arizona, which we got at a great price because it was still going through bad times. Meanwhile, HHC shared our vision and was committed to providing the capital needed to turn Douglas Ranch into the large-scale, master-planned community we wanted for the people of Phoenix.

El Dorado Holdings and JDM retained half ownership of the first phase of the project (about 3,300 acres) since we'd already entitled homebuilders who were in place and ready to go. Our part was to give HHC a soft landing in the market, introduce them to the players in Arizona, and help them negotiate things how Arizona does business. So, we

## 13. The Power of Thinking Big

continue to work with them in the development of those 3,300 acres. Now called Floreo, it will be the gateway into the giant Douglas Ranch master plan, which was renamed Teravalis.

We've already broken ground on the Floreo section of Teravalis and have crossed many hurdles and stepping stones necessary to break ground on the remainder. It's important to understand all this, because you'll discover in the third section of the book that your vision and planning are vital to creating your own Master Plan.

## CHAPTER FOURTEEN
# THE POWER OF THE MULTIPLE WIN

One of my driving principles is that everyone involved in a relationship, a business transaction, or a partnership should ultimately emerge as a winner. A "win-win" should always be the goal, no matter how lofty or trite or worn out those words may be to some readers. That's not to say that the "win-win" is easy. It's genuinely hard work, and it requires three things:

1. An honest desire to reach a suitable, workable solution.
2. An open mind that's able to consider options that were not previously on the table.
3. A willingness to compromise and accept slightly less than the "ideal" if need be.

The good news is, if you keep these three ideas in the forefront, you can create the "win-win" and, in many instances, the "win-win-win-win" or the multiple wins. I've participated in many multiple wins during my life and career. A specific instance with El Dorado Holdings is a deal I put together on the northeast intersection of 84th Street and Shea in Scottsdale, Arizona.

## 14. The Power of the Multiple Win

### The Church of the Nazarene

This parcel of land was owned by the Church of the Nazarene, and they wanted to sell. For fifteen years, a total of seven buyers had tried to rezone the property only to be turned down at the Scottsdale City Planning and Zoning mainly because the neighbors were actively opposed to any building on the property. They were also upset about the Catholic church that was immediately north of this property. Every time church services were held, cars were parked in the streets and driveways for blocks away.

As a result, the neighbors had refused to let the Catholic church get a building permit to build a new gymnasium for their youth. They withheld their support because of their animosity toward the church. Fearing even more traffic, the residents also didn't want to see apartment buildings or high-rise office buildings built on the property belonging to the Church of the Nazarene. For fifteen years, various parties tried to get the land rezoned, but the City of Scottsdale turned down applicants seven times because the neighbors fought every plan with all their might. As with any government position, they depend on votes during elections.

I firmly believed, however, that we could do something no one else had succeeded in doing. With that in mind, I approached the Church of the Nazarene and asked them, "If I can get it rezoned, will you sell it to me?"

They responded, "Yes, but good luck. Everyone else has been trying for almost two decades." We put the transaction in escrow depending on our ability to get the requested zoning.

With their blessing, I laid some important groundwork. I invested months of effort to create a "win-win-win" for every concerned party. I had countless neighborhood meetings, block parties, cookouts, and whatever else I could think of—all to draw in the neighbors. At these get-togethers, I asked them, "If I can figure out a way to get all the cars off the streets during church services, would you let the church build the gymnasium?" They said, "Yes, we would."

I went to see the parish priest and outlined my plan. I said, "I want to build an office complex on the land immediately south of you, with a guarantee to you that you can use the parking lots on Sundays, instead of using the neighborhood streets. If you agree with this plan, the neighbors will let you build the gymnasium for your youth program."

The priest got up from his desk and stood in front of me. "You've been sent by God," he said. "You've been sent here by God, and I can't believe it!" Then he gave me such a bear hug he almost squeezed the air out of me. He was excited when I showed him the plans I'd drawn up while working with the neighbors on the office complex idea. He was immediately on board.

When I was ready, I went to see Don Hadder, the head of planning and zoning for the City of Scottsdale. I said, "Don, I've got a new application here for you. It's the property on the northeast corner of 84$^{th}$ Street and Shea."

He couldn't believe what he was hearing. He said, "Mike, that's the worst piece of property in the whole town to try to rezone. It's right in the middle of the most organized neighborhood in our entire city. Don't make my life miserable by telling me you're going to try to do that. We've been through it too many times in my career."

## 14. The Power of the Multiple Win

I replied, "Don, I already have signatures here from every neighbor—all of them supporting my plan."

He looked at it and said, "I don't believe it! How in the world did you get them all to go along with you?"

I told him, "I've been working with them for over a year and a half. I've spent $300,000 on architectural fees to develop a concept that all of them could support."

It's difficult to design anything by committee, but I put together a group of the strongest, most vocal neighbors you can imagine. The core of the plan was to build some low-rise, professional office buildings. I allowed the committee to pick out the color palettes, the location of the buildings, and their size, shape, and structure. And I made sure none of the buildings obstructed their views of the McDowell Mountains.

We worked with Mike Davis and his architectural firm to make sure all the neighbors would be happy. I don't know how many hamburger barbecues we had in people's backyards in those eighteen months, but I walked into the City of Scottsdale with a signed application that was supported by every neighbor, without exception.

I was invited to come to the Catholic church at the groundbreaking ceremony for their new gymnasium. Not only that, but I was also invited up to the pulpit with my wife, Sheila, in front of the church where they gave me a round of applause. The turnaround in this neighborhood left me with a great sense of accomplishment.

Who were all the winners in this "win-win-win-win?" I won, of course, because I got to develop a piece of land that had been sitting dormant for years. The neighbors

## 14. The Power of the Multiple Win

won because they had input into what they all agreed was an outstanding project. Plus, their streets were no longer parking lots on Sundays. The neighboring Catholic church won. Not only were they building their new gymnasium and youth center, but their parishioners could also park in a lot next to the church, not blocks away. Also, I'd drafted a lifetime lease that allowed the parishioners to use the parking lot after hours and on weekends. Finally, the City of Scottsdale won because of the increased tax revenue these buildings generated.

Every party involved won a huge victory. The priest actually called me an "angel." I'm pretty sure I'm not an angel, but it felt mighty good to bring diverse groups with diverse interests together—and make every one of them a winner! It's the power of the multiple win on display!

# THE THIRD KEY: PERSONAL POWER

## CHAPTER FIFTEEN
# THE POWER OF VISION

You may have heard the old saying—originally from the Bible but often repeated—"Where there is no vision, the people perish." Of course, this saying is open to a lot of interpretation. Rather than head down that theological path, I'm going to create my own paraphrases as they relate to life and business:

*"Where there is no vision, the idea perishes."*
*"Where there is no vision, goals evaporate into nothingness."*
*"Where there is no vision, the great things that could have happened never materialize."*
*"A fool with a plan is better off than a genius without a plan."*

Visions are usually the result of one of three things: Deed, Need, or Greed. Inspiration can move you in either a positive or negative direction. Let's take a closer look.

- **Deed:** *Your vision may materialize because of something you or someone else has done.* For example, Dr. Martin Luther King Jr.'s vision of equality for all men was the outcome of generations of inequality and oppression. King wanted to see a nation in which people were judged by the content of their character rather than the color of their skin. It was a positive vision.

15. The Power of Vision

- **Need:** *Your vision could come to life because of something you believe others need.* In the 1950s, Dr. Jonas Salk envisioned the need for a vaccine to prevent polio—a dreaded disease. "Seeing" the need is what created his vision and ultimately led to a solution. Through the Salk vaccine and subsequent drugs, polio has virtually been eradicated from the earth.
- **Greed:** *Visions can also be negative.* Individuals can be driven by the desire for more money, more power, or more prestige. Entire nations can succumb to the lust for domination over other people and other lands. Visions based on greed may be successful for a while, but they are ultimately doomed to fail. To succeed, I believe, a vision needs to be meaningful.

## The Essential Components of a Vision

As the result of many years of personal experience, I have concluded that a meaningful vision is comprised of four key elements—or "Master Planning" steps:

1. Dreaming
2. Planning
3. Announcing
4. Executing

I remember when our newly elected president, John F. Kennedy, stated his vision for America's space program in his May 25, 1961, speech before a joint session of Congress. I recall the speech perfectly. He said, "I believe that this nation should commit itself to achieving the goal, before this decade is out, of landing a man on the moon and returning him safely to the earth."

15. The Power of Vision

General Charlie Duke, lunar module pilot of Apollo 16, and me at an El Dorado Holdings Celebrity Pheasant Hunt.

A salute from the moon from my dear friend and partner, General Charlie Duke, lunar module pilot of Apollo 16.

## 15. The Power of Vision

**Me, General Charlie Duke, lunar module pilot of Apollo 16, and Dan Adams — proud to call these two partners and friends.**

And it happened! Neil Armstrong and Edwin "Buzz" Aldrin, Jr., on the Apollo 11 mission, were the first humans to land the lunar module on the moon eight years later on July 20, 1969. Since then, a total of twenty-four people have gone to the moon. Only twelve of them touched their space-suit-clad feet on the surface of the moon—all of them Americans—including my good friend and great American Patriot, General Charlie Duke, the youngest of all the moonwalkers. Charlie wrote a great book entitled *Moonwalker*. I really think you would enjoy this book. I have had the pleasure of booking Charlie as a guest speaker at numerous events of mine. Here's the point: I'm virtually certain that President Kennedy didn't move directly to the "Announcing" stage of this vision without first consulting with many engineers and scientists—including the head

## 15. The Power of Vision

of NASA—regarding their views about the status of the "Dreaming" and "Planning" stages of the process. In other words, the President would not have announced the vision had he not first questioned whether the "Dreaming" stage had led to sufficient planning to determine whether or not the vision had a reasonable chance of becoming reality.

### Johnny Morris

My long-time friend, Johnny Morris, is a great example of putting all four components of vision into play. Johnny developed a passion for bass fishing as a young man and actually fished on the pro circuit for five years. Seeing a need for supplies for this growing sport, Johnny started selling bass plugs along the side of the road on the way to the lake. He got so busy that he convinced his father to allow him to set up shop from an eight-by-eight section in the back of his liquor store in Springfield, Missouri. It was the first Bass Pro Shop.

As Johnny's little enterprise grew, he was able to stock enough inventory to begin a sales catalog (announcing his products) which he distributed to customers in twenty states. Demand was so high he expanded with stores throughout the Midwest. To further his enterprise, Johnny introduced the industry's first "fish ready" boat, motor, and trailer package—the Bass Tracker®. His vision also included a massive headquarters store in Springfield, and, in 1981, he opened the Outdoor World National Headquarters Showroom, one of the largest retail stores in the world. It soon became Missouri's biggest tourist attraction. Because of its huge popularity, he opened additional Bass Pro Shops across the country. In 2017, Johnny purchased and merged

## 15. The Power of Vision

Cabela's 82 stores with his own 95 Bass Pro Shop locations, for a total of 177 locations.

In 1987, Johnny purchased property on Table Rock Lake which ultimately became Big Cedar Lodge—a 4,600-acre, first-class, nature-based resort and tourist destination. Since then, Johnny has continued to expand his landholdings to include a 10,000-acre nature park and Top of the Rock, a 462-acre property complete with a golf course, four restaurants, nature trail, and much more. I have so enjoyed Johnny's friendship over the years, and I look forward to every opportunity we have to hunt and fish together.

In 2017, Johnny developed Wonders of Wildlife National Museum & Aquarium in Springfield, a nonprofit educational conservation attraction comprised of an over 350,000 square-foot structure with a 1.5-million-gallon aquarium. He continued his vision of conservation when he successfully merged his largest outdoor hunting and fishing competitor, Cabela's, into his business plan. Now, Bass Pro Shops and Cabela's are under one company but operating independently.

Johnny's vision evolved from his love of the outdoors. His life story shows how he turned his passion for fishing and outdoor life into an empire that allowed him to share that vision with others. I would encourage everyone to examine their passions in life and pursue a vision in alignment with that passion.

## Our Vision for Floreo and Teravalis (Formerly Douglas Ranch)

The reason people often fail to fulfill their visions is that they process the four essential steps out of order. At

## 15. The Power of Vision

El Dorado Holdings, we are very deliberate in taking the essential steps one at a time—all in the correct order. I've already mentioned our vision was to create a very special master-planned community now known as Teravalis. I wish I could somehow show you what this community could become, but it would take a multitude of PowerPoint presentations, aerial tours, blueprints, detailed reports, and long meetings to reveal the full scope of the vision. Let's begin with the essentials: WHERE it is, WHY it needs to be, WHAT the benefits will be, and WHO will benefit from it.

The WHERE of Teravalis is about thirty-five miles west of Sky Harbor Airport, the central hub of the ever-growing Phoenix area. It's beautiful land that backs up to the White Tank Mountains. It's close enough to Phoenix to become a vital part of this vibrant metropolis, yet far enough away to allow for a ground-up, bottom-to-top development of a beautiful, planned community. Its location and the availability of abundant land and plentiful resources—combined with a well-designed plan—mean that nothing about it will be accidental or haphazard. Because of this, we will be able to realize our full and complete vision of a sustainable community.

There are several reasons WHY Teravalis will be significant. According to the State of Arizona Department of Administration, Maricopa and Pinal counties are expected to grow by two to five million people between now and 2030. When completed, Teravalis will include over 100,000 homes, 300,000 residents, and fifty-five million square feet of commercial space. It will provide an environmentally efficient and sustainable home for Arizona's future

## 15. The Power of Vision

residents. Every natural resource can be better utilized in a compact, well-designed, self-sufficient community. By "compact" I don't mean a crowded or poorly executed urban disaster. I mean that our exacting plan will allow for public and recreational land, office and industrial space, and educational and governmental use—all without the unnecessary sprawl of a typical unplanned city—complete with excellent educational facilities, shopping centers, medical centers and hospitals along with a variety of recreational areas and open space.

As to WHAT the benefits will be, may I simply suggest that you read on—because there are many. Some of them you could never imagine!

When it comes to WHO the beneficiaries will be, the short answer is "everyone who lives and works there, everyone in the Southwest United States, and every family that is building for the future." This vision is driven by need.

Critics question why we are so confident that Floreo and Teravalis will be a success when other recent master-planned developments—all of which are closer to central Phoenix than our planned project—have faced so many struggles. Why do our investors believe in our ability to pull off our plan? The answer, of course, lies in our vision.

There are two primary components to the original Douglas Ranch vision. The first part involves balance. We accomplished that through thoughtful design and dedicated land use. New innovations include the possibility of streets with the ability to charge electric cars while driving.

## 15. The Power of Vision

### Part One of Our Vision: Create Balance

In addition to creating residential neighborhoods, our master plan for Douglas Ranch (Teravalis) included over 7,000 acres set aside for open space, recreation areas, and a magnificent "Central Park" of New York City magnitude, as well as land for research facilities, a university campus, public and private schools, manufacturing and distribution centers, and federal, state, and local government buildings. How about those benefits?

There will be jobs for people and people for jobs. There will be that careful balance—essential to any neighborhood, community, city, county, state, or nation. Teravalis and Floreo will basically be a "city unto itself," while still being an extension of the town of Buckeye and a suburb of Phoenix. On top of that, there is already support for a new regional airport and light rail service. These are not just dreams—they're part of the vision and the master plan.

### Part Two of Our Vision: Create Access

The second part of our vision has to do with how Teravalis will connect with the rest of the world. In the real estate development world, this is known as "access."

Think about it. There's a reason that cities have historically been built on oceanfront property, along rivers, and in areas served by railroads and highways. Few major developments are miles away from seaports or transportation arteries. Remember, one of the reasons Maricopa became a viable project was because we created the infrastructure—the "Road to Maricopa," Amtrak rail service, and the development of public utilities. Plus, the land was affordable

## 15. The Power of Vision

and Interstate 10 was accessible, especially after State Route 347 was rebuilt as a four-lane divided highway.

But what about Teravalis? It's several miles from the segment of I-10 that links Phoenix and Los Angeles. It's nowhere near the Pacific Ocean, and there are no currently operating rail lines or spurs serving this new development. That's where our vision comes in and completes the picture.

### A New Highway

Let's go back in time for just a moment. Up until the 1950s, the cities in our nation were linked by a hodgepodge system of narrow two-lane highways, like the formerly undeveloped road that led to the tiny outpost known as Maricopa, Arizona. Then, along came President Dwight D. Eisenhower, a great military leader who served America so capably and valiantly during World War II. As President, he had a vision. Today, we call it the Interstate Highway System. You know it as I-10, I-35, I-40, I-90, I-94, I-55, I-75, I-95, I-78, I-88, I-81, I-84 . . . and so on.

Western U.S. Interstate system highlighting the I-11 Corridor.

## 15. The Power of Vision

Did you know that there are only two cities in the United States with populations of more than one million that are not connected by an interstate freeway? And those two cities are Phoenix and Las Vegas—two of the fastest growing metropolitan areas in the United States over the last twenty years.

According to some, those freeways haven't been built because many areas of fully developed Phoenix and its environs would have to be demolished to make room for the most direct route. That problem would be solved by creating a path from I-10 just west of Phoenix, leading through a place called Teravalis, and heading directly to Las Vegas. It's a "win-win" because we, along with several other private landowners, agreed to donate the land for the right-of-way, significantly reducing the cost of the project to taxpayers. It's a perfect example of a private-public partnership where everyone comes together. It will create jobs, provide a faster, safer route to Las Vegas, and reduce congestion on other freeways, such as on Interstate 17.

When the new interstate highway is completed, it will likely be known as Interstate 11. The part of the highway between Interstate 10 and the Arizona border with Nevada has been completed. The section between the border and north to Las Vegas is still in the planning stages. The concept of I-11 as a connection between Phoenix and Las Vegas has received Congressional approval, as many policy makers understand the benefits of a new Interstate Highway in the West. An expanded view of I-11 also envisions an extension north to Reno and the Pacific Northwest, as well as south to Mexico. It will eventually establish a trade route between

## 15. The Power of Vision

Canada and Mexico. Congestion will, as a result, be reduced on other Interstate freeways, especially in California. Already, more than thirty counties and communities have indicated their support for this significant project. Today, I-11 has Congressional approval to build a four-lane, divided highway with grade separation from the Arizona border through North Las Vegas.

Interstate 11 was part of the master plan for the original Douglas Ranch (Teravalis). Obviously, a vision this grand required its own Master Plan. To execute it, we had to draw several key partners into the many aspects of the program. The federal, state, and county governments all needed to buy into the plan. I worked with two supportive senators, Harry Reid from Nevada and Barbara Boxer from California, who supported the plan. Thankfully, much of this has happened. The full Interstate 11 is moving closer to reality.

It's been over fifteen years since Mary Peters asked me to take the project on. She assured me it was a one-dollar-a-year job. So far, they're more than fifteen dollars behind schedule. With interest rates the way they are, they'll probably owe me twenty bucks by now, maybe twenty-five! Seriously though, I'm happy to do anything to move the state of Arizona, and especially the Phoenix area, forward. Finishing Interstate 11 will be a "win-win-win" for the whole country.

All of us at El Dorado Holdings are problem solvers. We are very proud of the things we've achieved through our many successful partnerships in the past—in the metropolitan Phoenix area, in Tucson, and in Maricopa, among other projects. These partnerships have resulted in the entitlement or development of more than 50,000 single-family homesites

## 15. The Power of Vision

and in excess of 1,000 acres of industrial and commercial parcels. And that number continues to grow.

Floreo will join this list, in part because of the partnership we've formed with Howard Hughes Corporation, which has a long history of successful master-planned communities, including The Woodlands in Texas and Summerlin in Las Vegas. Our other partnership is with the outstanding and visionary firm of JDM Partnerships, LLC, headed by Jerry Colangelo, David Eaton, and Mel Shultz. Their past successes include Chase Field (where the Arizona Diamondbacks play ball), Footprint Center (home of the Phoenix Suns), Comerica Theatre (performing arts center), as well as the Cotton Business Center, The Wigwam Resort, Pagosa Lakes & Wyndham Pagosa Hotel, and two great golf courses at the Arizona Biltmore.

### A Word About Jerry Colangelo

Jerry Colangelo of JDM Partnerships has an outstanding reputation as a mover and shaker in Arizona. He was the general manager and eventual owner of the Phoenix Suns, as well as the founding partner of the Arizona Diamondbacks. He headed up the USA Basketball program—the teams that represent the United States in the Olympics—and is the Chairman of the Basketball Hall of Fame. At age twenty-six, he became the youngest general manager of the new NBA expansion team, the Phoenix Suns. He went on, in 1985, to become managing general partner of the new ownership for sixteen years. In the four Olympics he headed, he brought home gold medals each time.

In addition, Jerry has been involved as a board member

## 15. The Power of Vision

and advisor for Grand Canyon University since 2009. I was so pleased and overwhelmed to join the board of Grand Canyon in the fall of 2024. Hopefully, my experiences in life and business can be an asset to the current and future students at the University.

Under the guidance of President Brian Mueller, brought on in 2008, it's been transformed from a financially troubled university with a student body of around 800 and online students of 17,500, to boasting over 25,000 students on campus and an additional 100,000-plus online, making it the largest Christian university in the nation. Over two billion dollars has poured into infrastructure with classrooms, dormitories, sport facilities, and arenas. It's now an NCAA Division 1 ranked school and a contender in the NCAA Basketball National Tournament, "March Madness." The grand opening of The Colangelo College of Business was held January 9, 2019. The 150,000-square-foot building is the latest of a $12.8 billion academic infrastructure and technology renovation. A larger-than-life statue of Jerry stands at the front of the new facility. The left panel on the statue's base contains a famous quote from Jerry: "The community owes us nothing. We owe the community everything." There's also a tribute: "Jerry Colangelo is a man of integrity and loyalty, dedicated to faith, family, and community. A tireless and committed catalyst in the growth of the Phoenix community, he wants to be remembered for one thing—'He cared.'"

I'm very proud of my relationship with Jerry Colangelo and our partnership with JDM. Teravalis and Floreo will soon become a perfect example of how the Power of Partnerships

## 15. The Power of Vision

and the Power of Vision can help a new community to begin, grow, and evolve.

We at El Dorado Holdings have dreamed it, we have planned it, we have announced it to the world, and now, along with Howard Hughes Corporation, we are executing it. Vision in action!

**Jerry and Joan Colangelo – The only time you will ever see the Basketball Hall of Famer in a cowboy hat; 40 years and counting of a great friendship and partnership!**

## 15. The Power of Vision

**With Foster Friess (left) and Jerry Colangelo (center) — three men whose lives reflect a shared devotion to faith, family, community, and the power of generosity to change lives.**

# CHAPTER SIXTEEN
# THE POWER OF ENTHUSIASM

I know people who think life is a chore. They think work is a chore, marriage is a chore, and parenting is a chore. Everything for them is a chore. That's why I don't hang around with them. I avoid seeing and spending time with them because . . . well . . . being with them is a chore.

I want to associate with enthusiastic people. I want to work with enthusiastic people. Most of all, I'm lucky to be married to Sheila, who's an extremely enthusiastic person. It's not just my opinion. Ask anyone who knows her!

And I'm not the only one who feels that way. Psalm 118, verse 24 of the Bible says, "This is the day which the Lord has made; let's rejoice and be glad in it." In other words, "I'm awake, I'm alive, and I'm ready for today—no matter what it brings to me!" Whether or not people are aware of it, they enjoy being around others who start their day with those thoughts.

If you read this far, you know I love quotes by leaders from our time, as well as from the past. I have several framed quotes on display in my office. While I was considering the topic of enthusiasm, I found several quotes. Here's one of my favorites:

*"You can succeed at almost anything for which you have unbridled enthusiasm."*
-Zig Ziglar

## 16. The Power of Enthusiasm

These quotes are from Norman Vincent Peale, the founder of the Horatio Alger Award:

*"If you have zest and enthusiasm, you attract zest and enthusiasm. Life does give back in kind."*

*"There is a real magic in enthusiasm. It spells the difference between mediocrity and accomplishment."*

Here's another great thought from Earl Nightingale, the motivational speaker and author:

*"Creativity is a natural extension of our enthusiasm."*

And my last quote is from the great Winston Churchill:

*"Success consists of going from failure to failure without loss of enthusiasm."*

When someone comes to me wanting to invest in one of my properties—and there are many such people because they've heard about our successes—I'm very careful to make certain they're enthusiastic about the project itself, rather than simply enthusiastic about the prospect of making money.

For example, based on the success of Maricopa, there are people who wanted to invest in Douglas Ranch (Teravalis). Some of them were simply looking for a return on their investment, while others truly believed in what we were doing. It's the second group that adds value to a project because they will help "sell" it. They're the ones who will ensure the success of Floreo and Teravalis.

With that in mind, I have given some thought to "Examples of Enthusiasm"—what enthusiastic people think, believe, feel, and do every day.

## Examples of Enthusiastic People

**First:** *Enthusiastic people wake up in the morning with positive thoughts on their minds and uplifting attitudes in their hearts.* They see the sun shining, even if it's cloudy. They envision the day as filled with good things.

**Second:** *Enthusiastic people reinforce those thoughts and attitudes through a variety of behaviors and techniques.* Some may pursue a quiet time involving prayer, meditation, or the reading of scripture or other inspirational words. Others may go for a walk or run, perhaps while listening to upbeat music on their phones. Still, others may listen to motivational CDs, podcasts, audio books, or online programs during their commute—instead of the news or political banter. Some even become positive while listening to talk radio! To each his or her own.

**Third:** *Enthusiastic people are thankful.* They develop what's known as an "attitude of gratitude." This attitude is not situational. It's not simply the attitude they have when things are going well. Enthusiastic people find something to be thankful for, even when life doesn't seem to be going well. My belief is that all of us have something to be grateful for every day, whether we're rich or poor, married or single, employed or jobless, healthy or in need of physical, emotional, or spiritual healing. Here's one of my favorite quotes from author and teacher Brian Tracy:

> *"Develop an attitude of gratitude, and give thanks for everything that happens to you, knowing that every step forward is a step toward achieving something bigger and better than your current situation."*

## 16. The Power of Enthusiasm

This is an important aspect of enthusiasm, so let's look a little deeper. Maybe you feel that you have little to be thankful for. If that's the case, I strongly suggest you make a list of your blessings—not just in your head, but also on paper. I've actually done this for years, and it's helped me get through the darkest times in my life. I'm not going to share my entire list with you because such lists are highly personal. Yours will be different from mine. But here are some basics to help inspire your first list:

- I'm thankful for the people I love and for those people who love me. *(I hope you can include your parents, siblings, spouse, children, and friends on this list.)*
- I'm thankful that I live in a free country. *(I don't know where you live, but I hope you live in freedom too.)*
- I'm thankful for the men and women who fought to protect that freedom.
- I'm thankful I was able to achieve the level of education I have—no matter what that level may be. *(I firmly believe that many great things have happened through those with a sixth-grade education as well as those with multiple PhDs.)*
- I'm thankful for books and my ability to read them. *Great ideas live on the pages of great books.*
- I'm thankful for the people with whom I work—my team, my advisors, my investors, and my customers. *(Not many people are thankful for their lawyers, brokers, or accountants, but I am!)*
- Ultimately, I'm thankful for life. I'm also thankful that I'm still in good health. *As my Jewish friends say, "L'chaim." It means "to life," but it also means "to your health and well-being." Now that's positive!*

**Fourth:** *Enthusiastic people spread their enthusiasm to others.* Share it! I'm sure you've been in situations where someone who was depressed and negative brought everyone else down to his or her level. As Zig has said: *"Some people can brighten up a room just by leaving it."*

In another conversation with Zig, he told me, "Some people look like someone licked all the red off their candy." I could definitely understand what he was telling me.

Well, the opposite is also true. Enthusiasm is contagious. You can impact the lives of others with your positive attitude. Your side benefit is that making others more positive will increase your own enthusiasm.

**Fifth:** *Enthusiastic people end their day with gratitude and positive thoughts.* I generally don't watch the news on television at night. There's too much nasty stuff going on in the world. Instead, I affirm my love for my wife, and I end my day by reading something positive. (You guessed it . . . usually the Bible).

I apply the power of enthusiasm on a daily basis, and it works. It's a key element of my Master Plan. My enthusiasm rubs off on my team members at El Dorado Holdings, it rubs off on our investors, and it even rubs off on people who are initially opposed to our objectives.

Zig was always reminding me to listen to the positive ideas, not the negative. "Garbage In—Garbage Out." Be selective to the good, constructive and moral ideas. Feed the mind and soul with these ideas.

Enthusiasm can change the mind and heart of the most stubborn people on earth!

## CHAPTER SEVENTEEN
# THE POWER OF INTEGRITY

Few things in life are more important than an individual's reputation. When I meet new people, I generally know something about them ahead of time because their reputations have preceded them. Friends and associates will say either, "Watch out for him. He doesn't have a very good reputation." or "You can trust her—she really has integrity." I'm guessing you've heard similar things about people you've met even before you've met them.

The problem is that once people have ruined their reputation, it's almost impossible to get it back. We may try to overlook someone's flawed integrity, but we never really get over it, do we? Building a good reputation and becoming known as a person of integrity takes a long time, and it can all disappear in an instant, maybe never to be regained.

When I hire someone, I'm more interested in their integrity than their skills. When I establish a relationship with a new investor, I'm more attuned to their integrity than to how much money they have in the bank. The proverbs of King Solomon offer sage advice on this topic:

> "Whoever walks in integrity walks securely, but whoever takes crooked paths will be found out."
> (Proverbs 10:9, NIV)

## 17. The Power of Integrity

The following story is a demonstration of integrity—of doing the right thing at great personal cost:

### Glenn Stearns

Glenn Stearns is a good friend of mine. He founded Stearns Lending, headquartered in Newport Beach, California. Glenn was inducted into the Horatio Alger Association in 2011, another of my friends to receive this honor.

At the age of fourteen, Glenn got his sixteen-year-old neighbor pregnant. Marriage at such a young age was not a great idea, but the girl had the baby and Glenn had integrity. As a result, he worked hard to support his baby all her life. That baby is now the president of one of his companies. Wouldn't it be wonderful if every man who fathered a baby did everything possible to follow through on his obligations?

### Characteristics That Apply to People with Integrity

- **Truthfulness:** *Persons of integrity speak the truth in a loving way.* While correcting or admonishing someone, they always include words of encouragement. They don't share every bitter thought and suggestion, no matter how painful. They are not cruel. That's why I added "in a loving way."

- **Consistency:** *Persons of integrity don't change the way they act from day to day.* They never surprise people with unexpected unpleasantries. They're always consistent. I can actually predict with nearly 100% accuracy how the people in my business

### 17. The Power of Integrity

and my life are going to react to certain situations. That's because I surround myself with people whose lives are consistent with their values and beliefs.

- **Follow-through:** *Persons of integrity do everything possible to avoid making promises they can't keep, and they follow through on promises made.* When Deb Bricker or Denise Organ or someone else on my staff promises something, I know they'll come through or have a valid reason why they can't. Follow-through begins with the commitments one makes. My definition of commitment is this: *"The ability to carry out a resolution, long after the mood in which it was made has passed."* Lots of people have good ideas, but they don't always see them through. They don't have stick-to-itiveness.

There've been so many times we at El Dorado Holdings could have quit because of the obstacles we faced. I think about the road to Maricopa—the story I told you earlier. We were mocked by the press. They called our project "The Road to Nowhere." The temptation to abandon an idea that is ridiculed is often overwhelming. But people with ideas, with vision, and with goals are often ridiculed. That's certainly true in the world of land development and it's true with some of our ongoing developments including Floreo, El Dorado Bella Vista, El Dorado Arizona Farms, and Merrill Ranch "Montanero."

But we can't quit. There are a lot of people who have put their trust—and their hard-earned money—in El Dorado Holdings. My team and I have to see it through. We have to see it become successful. If we are asking someone

## 17. The Power of Integrity

to believe in our ideas, to trust in us, we have to follow through. There's no option to stop.

I'm sure many of my team members over the last forty years might say I haven't been easy to work with. That may be true, but I believe it's because I expect a lot of myself and, in turn, I expect a lot of my them. A strong work ethic is evident in each and every one of my team members.

People often ask me if a recent trip was business or pleasure. I always respond, "Yes," and refer them to a favorite writing by author James Michener:

*"The Master*
*In the art of living*
*Draws no distinction between*
*His work and his play,*
*His labor and his leisure,*
*His mind and his body,*
*His education and his recreation,*
*His love and his religion.*
*He hardly knows which is which.*
*He simply pursues his vision of excellence*
*Through whatever he is doing*
*And leaves it to others*
*To determine whether he is working or playing.*
*To himself he is always doing both."*

Follow-through is at the core of integrity. As you approach your commitments, you have to be prepared to do everything in your power to see them through.

## The Need for Ethical Leadership

Sadly, there seem to be fewer people with integrity than there were when I was growing up. Ethics have been "grayed over." They've been blurred beyond recognition. The permanent values in life seem to be sacrificed on the altar of immediate gratification today. It's one of the primary reasons I threw my support behind the establishment of the Zig Ziglar Center for Ethical Leadership at Southern Nazarene University in Bethany, Oklahoma.

Southern Nazarene University (SNU) is a Christian university that emphasizes the importance of service to its students, whether to the church, the community, the nation, or the world. What's Zig Ziglar's connection? You could say it goes back to the 1980-81 basketball season, when the college was still called Bethany Nazarene. Coach Loren Gresham led the team to the National Association of Intercollegiate Athletics (NAIA) national championship game, during which they played the University of Alabama-Huntsville. Coach Gresham inspired his team to greatness using video recordings of Zig Ziglar's inspiring talks. His plan worked! The college won 86 to 85 in overtime. It was also the first NAIA championship game that went into overtime. This small, Christian college took home the trophy.

You may have noticed that I, too, have been inspired by Zig Ziglar. Because of that and because I have a place in my heart for both the school and the state of Oklahoma, I decided to help fund the Zig Ziglar Center for Ethical Leadership, as well as raising funds from others. Although the university's leadership wanted to name the Center after Sheila and me, we preferred to honor the man who had impacted our lives in so many ways.

## 17. The Power of Integrity

I believe that ethics—integrity—can and must be passed on to the next generation. Helping make that happen is an important part of my Master Plan. Today, the Center serves new generations of students who will benefit from the ethical lessons I learned as a young man, and these young people will impact the world with what they have learned.

If you don't believe how important integrity is to me and El Dorado Holdings, why not hear it from a woman who has worked with me for over three decades? I've mentioned her name before as one of my most trusted employees—Deb Bricker.

### A Word About Integrity from Deb Bricker

*As you know from reading this book, I have been associated with Mike for many years. As a matter of fact, I was his first employee in El Dorado Holdings, joining him on day two, now almost forty years ago. I'd moved down from Wyoming and had just lost a job working for a small developer. The man I'd been working for had heard about a couple of guys who were just starting out. So, I interviewed with Mike and Monty Ortman, his partner. They hired me the same day.*

*Mike had basically nothing back then. They had one piece of property in escrow. In fact, the first ten years were pretty tough. I was raising two small children alone, but they always made sure I had a paycheck, even if they didn't take one themselves. I didn't have much money, so Mike also funded my first investment in El Dorado. He didn't have to do that, but he wanted me to use that money to go forward. Now I'm in on almost every investment deal, I'm secretary-treasurer of the corporation, and I sit on the board of directors. Mike's*

## 17. The Power of Integrity

*relationship with me has evolved from employer to mentor to friend ... and now I consider him family.*

*The reason? Mike is everything he says he is and everything he wants to be. All the principles in this book are more than theory. They come from his firsthand life experience. Over the years, I've watched Mike give back to others, many times when it was least expected. Mike takes his bond with his investors, team members, and friends to a different level. It's the diligence that he puts into establishing relationships up front, then the loyalty and connection that really last forever.*

*For example, years ago, El Dorado was in the process of buying two pieces of farmland known as "Homestead Village North" and "Homestead Village South" in what is now Maricopa, Arizona. While putting together a proposal to raise money from our investors for these two properties, Mike received an offer from a homebuilder to purchase the land for tens of millions of dollars more than the purchase price. Closing this deal would have made Mike a very wealthy man. He could have retired instantly, shut down the company, let all of his employees go (including me), and lived the "good life" from that day forward.*

*Instead, he moved ahead and offered the deal to our investors, and they received the bulk of the profits instead of Mike and El Dorado. He may have lost millions in this deal, but he gained trust, dedication, and respect from all of us who admire him. A man of true integrity!*

# CHAPTER EIGHTEEN
# THE POWER OF FORGIVENESS

Years ago, a great NBA player and a great NBA owner had a huge falling out. Cruel words were spoken by the player. Animosity grew. The player denigrated the owner for trading him to another team, yet the owner remained silent. The player was Charles Barkley. The owner was Jerry Colangelo of the Phoenix Suns. While I know "Sir Charles," and realize he is a tremendous athlete, Jerry is a good friend and business associate of mine.

In 2004, the relationship between the two men was restored. I can't claim to know why Charles decided to make amends with Jerry. But I recall reading in the *Arizona Republic* that Jerry said words to the effect that "Because I'm a Christian and claim to be a follower of Jesus, I have to live up to my beliefs." I also attended an event during which Jerry was "roasted" by associates and athletes alike. Charles was there, and the beautiful restorative energy between the two men was a testament to the power of forgiveness. This is something to which we all should aspire, and I thank Charles and Jerry for demonstrating it to all of us.

The banner bearing Barkley's number was added to the Ring of Honor at US Airways Center (now Footprint Center), and Charles, who lives in Phoenix, regularly attends Suns' games. Mutual forgiveness has made the lives of two men better.

## 18. The Power of Forgiveness

But what happens when the stakes are huge, when the wrongs committed by one party are almost inconceivable? A friend reminded me of the true story of Corrie Ten Boom. He heard her tell it firsthand.

### Corrie Ten Boom

Corrie and her family were watchmakers who lived in Holland during the dark days of the Nazi invasion. Though not Jewish, Corrie, her sister, their father, and several other family members got involved in the "underground," hiding Jewish friends and neighbors in their house until they could be transported to safety.

Their activities quickly caught the attention of the occupying forces, and Corrie and her family were arrested. She and her sister, Betsy, were sent to Ravensbruck Concentration Camp where Betsy died. Corrie was eventually released as the result of a clerical error.

After the war's end, Corrie went on extensive speaking tours to tell her story. She traveled without incident to several countries around the globe until one day she spotted a man she instantly recognized. He walked up to her after her speech and confessed that he was, in fact, one of the German guards who had treated her so despicably in prison.

Corrie was stunned into silence. She had no idea how to respond to this man. Then, without prompting and with a huge lump in her throat and tears in her eyes, she said three simple words, "I forgive you." The man broke down and cried uncontrollably.

That kind of forgiveness is difficult, and for many of us, it would be impossible. But I believe Corrie Ten Boom was modeling her life after the ultimate example of forgiveness.

## 18. The Power of Forgiveness

As He was dying on the cross on a hillside outside Jerusalem some 2,000 years ago, Jesus Christ looked down on the men who had driven spikes through His hands and feet and had placed a crown of thorns upon His head, and He said, "Father, forgive them, for they don't know what they are doing."

That kind of forgiveness is nearly beyond human capability, my friends. The lesson is simple: even if forgiveness is extremely difficult, it is still important. I can think of four reasons why we should do our best to practice forgiveness.

### Four Reasons to Practice Forgiveness

**First**: *Anger can eat a person alive, while it has little effect on the person with whom he or she is angry.* I really believe that anger can be a killer. It raises blood pressure, disrupts the digestive system, and impacts the body in many other negative ways. If you don't believe me, ask your doctor or a psychologist.

**Second:** *Forgiveness makes a way for a new beginning.* I know people who have eventually become best friends with people they've forgiven. Old wounds can be healed.

**Third**: *When you forgive someone, you're taking the "high road."* You're not sinking to a level that may have angered you in the first place. You can be confident that you've done the right thing.

**Fourth:** *You will actually sleep better when you forgive others and let go of the past.* You'll stop holding on to those negative thoughts at night.

## 18. The Power of Forgiveness

### How Offering Forgiveness Worked for Me

I had the opportunity to forgive and erase the past with a man named Ed Jessup. I'm glad I did! I met Ed during my early years with Merck. I had to hire a salesman, and that guy was Ed.

Ed is the most natural salesman I've ever met in my life. He has more raw ability and talent for selling than anyone I've ever known. But he started drinking too much, which created a lot of drama and mistrust between us, so we parted ways. Years later, I ran into Ed by accident at a service station in West Texas, where he had relocated.

He said, "Mike, if you ever decide to open up an operation in West Texas, please call me. I want to be a part of it. I really enjoyed working with you for the years I lived in Oklahoma. I know we had some tough times when I went through my divorce, but I've remarried. I've come to know the Lord. I've quit drinking, I've married a wonderful Christian girl, and my life is completely different. If you ever give me another chance, I won't disappoint you." I listened and pondered what he said. *Could I believe him?* I wondered. *Could I forgive him?*

At lunch that same day, I ran into my cousin, Nolan Chandler, who had been one of the top salesmen in the field of animal health in West Texas for over thirty years. He gave me the same story: "If you ever decide to open up anything here in West Texas, let me know." It instantly occurred to me that something exciting was coming together!

I called James Walsh, a Merck representative living in Lubbock, Texas, and I said, "James, is there any way I can get you to travel to Amarillo tonight? I have an idea."

## 18. The Power of Forgiveness

James drove to meet me, we had dinner, and I talked about the possibility of starting a new branch, a Tufts & Son Western Division, based in Amarillo. I asked him if he would consider becoming the general manager. I told him, "I think we could get Nolan Chandler and Ed Jessup to join with us."

He was visibly excited. "My gosh, that would be powerful! They're the top two salesmen in all of West Texas."

The four of us met the next day for breakfast. Everyone thought it was a great idea. I didn't even have to get John Tufts to buy into this—and that amazes me to this day. John had complete confidence in my leadership.

I called John on the way back to Oklahoma City and announced, "You won't believe this, but I was delivering some products in West Texas, and I ran into Ed Jessup. I also ran into Nolan Chandler, a tremendous salesman. I called James Walsh from Merck and asked him to have dinner with me last night. We all met for breakfast this morning and decided that we'd open a new branch in Amarillo, Texas."

John said, "Mike, that sounds great."

And we were off and running. James Walsh was a brilliant manager. Ed and Nolan put us on the map. James, his new assistant, Sue Buescher, and the two salesmen continued to grow the company. We eventually opened offices in Clovis, New Mexico, Garden City, Kansas, and Hereford, Texas. I owned it all with John Tufts. As it grew even more, I brought in Roy McKay, whom I'd known since third grade in Roswell, New Mexico—we were inseparable growing up. Roy became a third investor with John and me, primarily to have additional operating capital.

## 18. The Power of Forgiveness

But it all began when Ed Jessup approached me and told me his life had changed. I chose to trust him, believe him, and forgive him—and our Master Plan began to grow and evolve. It was the right move, and I've never regretted that decision.

**My best friend, Roy McKay and his wife Charlotte, back in the day. I set up their first date.**

# CHAPTER NINETEEN
# THE POWER OF PERSISTENCE

*"When obstacles arise, you change your direction to reach your goal; you do not change your decision to get there."*
—Zig Ziglar

I've always admired people who persist in reaching their goals. I can think of several examples from the past. One that immediately comes to mind is Thomas Alva Edison. I've heard that he tried more than 2,000 different substances for the filament in the electric light bulb before he found one that worked dependably. I've even heard that he failed 3,000, 5,000, and even 10,000 times during his quest. He wisely said (and I paraphrase here) that every failure brought him one step closer to success. Think about it. Edison didn't change his decision to reach his goal—he simply changed his direction 2,000 (or 3,000, 5,000, even 10,000) times. What persistence! Again, I reiterate: the ability to carry out leads to success.

Winston Churchill's quote also comes to mind: *"Never, never, never give up."* Churchill had a major role in guiding the United Kingdom and the free world through World War II. It was one of the darkest times in history. Persistence, combined with focused passion, is a great formula for success. Let's see how persistence paid off for some of the people I know today.

## 19. The Power of Persistence

### Jim Winjum

Jim Winjum combined his love for the outdoors with his pursuit of business from an early age. He grew up in the great outdoors of north central Montana and spent his youth hunting, fishing, hiking, and camping. After attending Montana State University, he graduated with a degree in mechanical engineering. But rather than looking for employment in aerospace and aviation, Jim remained in Montana. He started working with a small boot company called Schnee's Boots and Shoes. Jim (and his parents) may have wondered if he was wasting his education, but he knew what he wanted to do and doggedly pursued it. Schnee's was a small company, which gave Jim the opportunity to learn every aspect of the business. He designed the company's first rubber-bottom/leather-top PAC-style boot and went on to manage its production and marketing. When the company was sold, Jim joined with two other partners to start a company of his own. It was the birth of Kenetrek Boots.

The first several years of the business were a challenge because of the recession. It was extremely difficult to market new boots when retail sporting stores were struggling to just keep their doors open. Jim credits his passion for hunting and the "never give up" attitude he gained through that experience for surviving the tough initial years of his new company. His persistence paid off. Eventually, Kenetrek began to grow and continues to do so today. Learning from his own hunting experiences about the footwear necessary for comfort and stability in rugged country, Jim has consistently improved Kenetrek's boot line. In addition to sportsmen's boots, Kenetrek has answered the need of other professions, from the Lineman Extreme boot for linemen and other outdoor workers to the Wildland Fire boot for wildland firefighters. The company even produces orthopedic and military footwear. Jim remains an avid sportsman and is grateful his passion for the outdoors led him to a successful career where he helped others enjoy that same passion.

## Jane and Wade Askew

Jane Askew and her husband, Wade, are another example of persistence. They were a retired couple living in Maricopa while it was still a town of fewer than 500 residents. When we announced our plan to build the "Road to Nowhere," Jane immediately became one of our most ardent and vocal supporters. She wasn't that interested in our plan to develop residential neighborhoods. She simply thought the two-lane road linking Maricopa with the rest of the world was horribly unsafe. She saw every mile as dangerous and hated to travel on it.

Jane became a serious and involved advocate of State Route 347. She scheduled her own neighborhood meetings and attended those held by others. She planned get-togethers over coffee, and she wrote an endless stream of letters to people of position and power. She was one of the most involved and persistent community activists I'd ever met. And she did all this from her wheelchair. Nothing could stop her!

Sadly, Jane never lived to witness the outcome of her persistence. She died in a horrific automobile accident on the old, unimproved road before it was finished. How I would

## 19. The Power of Persistence

have loved to have seen Jane Askew at the ribbon cutting for the road she fought to have built! We honored her memory by naming the new park we built in Maricopa after her. It's called—appropriately—Jane Askew Park.

### Valley Christian High School

The power of persistence also applies to the story of Valley Christian High School in Chandler, Arizona. I promise you; this story has an upbeat ending!

Several years ago, I bought 140 acres on Ray Road and Fifty-Sixth Street from an investor in California who was in financial trouble and was losing the property. The parcel was zoned for industrial use, and the city of Chandler had made it clear to every developer that it would never be rezoned for residential use. I knew it would take years and years to develop it as an industrial property. In the meantime, I would let the land sit idle.

About the time I considered buying the property, some parents of students who attended Valley Christian High School approached me and asked to help them find land for a new school. They knew I was in the real estate business and had a soft spot in my heart for education. They hoped I could find some reasonably priced land for their new campus.

I immediately thought of the land I was looking at and said, "You know, I'm purchasing 140 acres at 56th and Ray."

They were excited. "That would be a perfect location. But we only need fifteen acres."

I thought for a moment and told them, "If I can get that property rezoned to residential, I can sell it to homebuilders.

## 19. The Power of Persistence

If I can sell it for more than I'm paying, I will use the excess money to reduce your cost."

I then approached the City of Chandler with my plan. They told us they were not against it. In fact, they were *very much* against it. The mayor was opposed to it, the city council was opposed to it, and everyone on the staff was opposed to it.

We began lobbying the city council, and we told them how desperately the school needed this property. I hired a zoning attorney by the name of Paul Gilbert from Beus Gilbert McGroder, one of the very best law firms in Phoenix. Paul is the top zoning attorney in Arizona, maybe the best in the Western hemisphere. On the big night—the night of the zoning hearing—we showed up with nearly 200 parents and most of the students who attended the school. Many of the parents were prominent members of the community, and all of them were Chandler voters!

I did not know what was going to happen, except that they had put us as the last item on the agenda. To make sure we could keep all the students and parents there, I kept ordering pizzas and Pepsis which I had delivered to the parking lot. Everyone was enjoying the pizza party, so they all hung with us outside.

Finally, it was our turn. Just minutes before midnight, we all marched into the chambers in a quiet, orderly, and respectful manner. The room was so packed with parents and students that it was standing room only.

Going into the meeting earlier that night, Paul Gilbert whispered, "Mike, we need to withdraw our case. We're going to go down in flames."

## 19. The Power of Persistence

I answered, "Paul, I want to continue."

He said, "Boy, I should have taken on this case by the word instead of by the hour."

I put out my hand, shook his, and said, "You've got a deal, Paul. I'll pay you by the word."

When we were all in the room, representatives of the city got up and made their case. They presented lots of slides and gave every reason in the world why the property should not be rezoned as residential. Believe me, they eloquently stated their case. They were prepared!

When they finished and sat down, the mayor said, "I believe the applicant now will be represented by Mr. Gilbert. He has been asked to make the presentation." He continued, "Mr. Gilbert, would you please come to the front of the room?"

As Paul walked to the microphone, one of the city council members, Lowell Huggins, a barber in Chandler, said, "Mr. Mayor, I think everybody here knows the issue. We've all been briefed on it many, many times. Every city council member knows the issues. We've heard from the city. We know their side and they have presented it very well. Meanwhile, we know what the applicant wants to do with this property." Then he stunned everyone by saying, "I make the motion that we approve the applicant's plan as presented."

Immediately, Jay Tibshraeny, a council member who later became mayor, said, "I second that motion," and he called for a vote.

I was shocked. The mayor was shocked. "What? There's a motion?" He was visibly annoyed because he was opposed to our plan.

But he had no choice in the matter because the motion had been made and seconded and the vote was called for. The secretary read the motion, the vote was taken, and our plan passed five to two!

After the meeting, I went up to Paul and said, "I am sure glad we agreed to pay you by the word." Although he'd worked very hard on the case, he had never said one word during the council session. As a man of honor, he never charged me one cent for his services.

Paul still laughs about it. He once told me, "Mike, I paid the price later on. I got beat up for years in the City of Chandler, because they still remember that case and hold me responsible for it."

I said, "Paul, we thank you and the school thanks you. I know they appreciate your hard work on their behalf. As you know, all of my profit from the sales of the residential land went to Valley Christian High School. The only profit I'll make will be from the ten acres of commercial land I have remaining."

Paul Gilbert is one of the finest zoning attorneys in Arizona. He remains a close friend—and a demonstration of the power of persistence.

This story shows how the union of vision, planning, and persistence can transform the impossible into a reality!

## Glenn Stearns – One of America's Greatest Businessmen and Salesmen

"Never give up" reminds me of another good friend of mine, Glenn Stearns. He's been an investor of mine for well over two decades. I mentioned him briefly in the chapter

## 19. The Power of Persistence

on Integrity, but there's more to his remarkable story. Most people choose to run away from a raging fire, but Glenn chose to run directly into one—with positive results.

In 1989, Glenn founded a mortgage company in California with a partner whose family had loaned him $100,000. Glenn and his partner grew their company even through tough times. But in 1998, when the business was really struggling, Glenn's partner offered to sell his share to him at a ridiculously low price, giving Glenn full ownership.

When the real estate boom hit, Glenn's company suddenly was writing $250 million a month in new business. His success, however, was short-lived. The mortgage market started to crumble, and Glenn began receiving letters from his investors who were becoming increasingly protective of their investments. They wanted Glenn to repurchase the loans.

Glenn said to himself, "Uh-oh! Something is happening here!" In December 2006, he immediately tightened his loan guidelines. In January 2007, he lost 50 percent of his revenue in loan value, and he got even more conservative. More letters came, with more attempts from lenders to have their loans repurchased.

By September 2007, Glenn's company had lost 85 percent of its revenue and only had $19 million in funding. That sounds like a lot of money, but not when stakeholders in $60 million in loans want their loans repurchased and another $30 million in assets are trapped in credit lines and can't be sold to anyone. On top of all that, there were class-action suits being filed against Glenn and his company.

Glenn's company wasn't the only one facing this drama. The "bubble" had burst. The world of lending was collapsing. Glenn was sure his company was going under.

## 19. The Power of Persistence

"I need a plan of action," he thought and decided to connect several of his mentors. They advised him, "Don't hide. Address the issues. Approach your creditors and be honest. Talk honestly to banks." Armed with that advice, Glenn went to Wall Street. He went to banks and other lenders to whom he owed money, offering them ten cents on the dollar. The alternative was bankruptcy. To the person... to the company... every one of his creditors said they would work with him. They allowed him to "fight to live." In the process of fighting, Glenn reduced his enormous office from 40,000 square feet to only 8,000 square feet. He tore down one hundred cubicles and paid to have them removed. Yes, he actually had to pay to give them away!

This is where Glenn "walked into the raging fire instead of running away from it." Several of his largest competitors in the mortgage industry were also going bankrupt. They had well-established offices with talented people in their stable—people with ten, fifteen, or more years of experience. That gave Glenn an idea.

He went to his landlord, and said, "Wait! Let's keep the cubicles!" He then paid to buy them back. He actually purchased them a second time! Next, he arranged desks and cubicles in neat rows and put a computer monitor on each desk—not the actual computers, only the monitors. Just enough to give the *impression* that the business was poised to take off.

Armed with a plan, he went to the office managers of his competitors and said, "I want to offer jobs to your very best people."

They told him he was crazy. "We're letting everyone go

## 19. The Power of Persistence

and we're shutting down. How can you think about hiring in this economy?"

But Glenn was persistent! He not only reopened his office, but he also opened other offices wherever he could find top-performing people. He saw the situation as a once-in-a-lifetime opportunity to find the best team ever. A week later, those desks were filled. His strategy was to go back to the basics. No more subprime mortgages—only conventional ones—and the best team around.

By November 2007, Glenn had offices in five cities. In 2008, Glenn's company had its best year since 1989. In 2009, he beat all of 2008 in just a single month. Stearns Lending grew to be the number one independent mortgage company in the country, writing well over a *billion* dollars of business a month!

Glenn Stearns accomplished this by seizing that once-in-a-lifetime opportunity, focusing on the positives instead of the negatives, and believing in the best people. All that and adding an extra helping of persistence!

But the story doesn't end there. Glenn's spirit of persistence not only helped him in business and his financial battles, but also in his battle with health issues. Glenn tells his own story here:

## 19. The Power of Persistence

**Mindy and Glenn Stearns horsin' around at Bell Cross Ranch.**

In 2011, I was inducted into the Horatio Alger Association. I had sold the majority interest in my company right around that time. My life was beyond great. I thought I had it made. On my fiftieth birthday, my wife threw this big party for me. I believe you were there, Mike. Everyone did a roast while I sat in a little jail cell. But I wasn't feeling well. Here I had what I thought was all the money in the world. What could go wrong?

Right after the Horatio Alger event, I was having dinner with Dick Cheney at his house in Virginia: Dick, Lynn, Liz, Mindy, and myself. I said I wasn't feeling well. Dick said, "I'm feeling great!" (He had a new heart.) I said, "Man, I don't." He advised me, "Well, go see my doctor." So, I went to George Washington University Hospital in Washington, D.C. and met his doctor. They took me into the hospital and basically shook

## 19. The Power of Persistence

me upside down. The next day the doctor said, "We're going to put you under because there's a little something I don't like."

I thought, "Okay, well then go in and do a biopsy." But I never understood what that meant. It never occurred to me what a biopsy really is. The next day I'm on the gurney. Mindy flew home, so I'm by myself. I'm a little nervous to go under, and in walks the doctor. "Yep, just what I thought. It's squamous cell carcinoma."

I remember thinking in my head, "Carcinoma. Carcinoma. That's not a good word." Then he looked me in the eye and said, "Yeah. Cancer." Suddenly, my world went straight down this dark little tunnel.

The doctor sensed my feelings and said, "No, no, no. This is curable. There is a fifty to fifty-five percent cure rate."

Wow. A 50/50 chance of survival. That's basically a coin toss. I was in shock. I remember at that moment thinking about my kids. My little kids. I thought, "I just can't leave these kids. I need to be around to imprint. To see them grow. To be a part of their lives." As I lay there, I also thought, "All the money in the world now isn't worth my health. It doesn't matter what I have. I'd give it all up."

So, I fought the fight. I ended up taking the chemotherapy and radiation. I lost forty-five pounds. According to Mindy, I was in so much pain, I laid a lot of times on the floor. I don't remember it at all. I was in a morphine haze. But I got through it and came out the other side.

Before that dark day, I was making a lot of money and feeling cocky. I went from thirteen billion to twenty-six billion in sales. We were killing it. I felt like I couldn't lose. I was living the high life.

## 19. The Power of Persistence

*Now, I saw the world so much differently. The money, toys, all those kinds of things didn't matter. My world was no longer defined by who I was in a mortgage company. When I got cancer, I came out the other side and thought, "Why do I do all this?" So, I sold 70 percent to Blackstone, and I bought a huge boat. It was an amazing boat with a helicopter and landing pad. I took my kids out of school and asked my son, who was about to go to college, if he would forego college. I asked him if he would be a deckhand on my boat. We went around the world.*

*Before that time in my life, I never sat down for breakfast, lunch, or dinner with my kids. I never did those family things. It was always about slaying the dragons and building the company. It was always about climbing a higher mountain. So now, every day, whether we were in Indonesia or the Maldives or Thailand, it didn't matter. We spent each dinner together, and it was a wonderful feeling to just share moments with my family.*

*I went to see my doctor every six months for a checkup. Every time he'd come in to see me at the end of my appointments, he'd say, "Hey, Glenn, how you doing? Everything looks fine. You're good." He would calm me down and then off I'd go for another six months.*

*After one of my appointments, after I got my scan and blood tests, I was actually a little anxious. I came home at six o'clock and there was a phone call from the doctor. He left a message. "I need to talk to you." When I finally got in touch with him, he said, "We see something very little on the scan again." This was after four years of being cancer free.*

*You'd think by now I would've learned that this is a way*

## 19. The Power of Persistence

*that God brings you back to reality—to understand what's important.*

*I went back in. They did another scan and another biopsy, and sure enough, it was cancer again. They decided to cut it out. They had done new work in immunotherapy, so they cut my epiglottis off.*

*I'm now in a new place in my life. I'm not sure what I can eat and what I can do anymore. I'm trying and learning. I'm back at it, and thankful again, being grateful for what's around me. I hope this time it sticks because I am not planning on being sick anymore.*

*It's very basic. It's about putting our phones down, being present, being grateful. We need to do things that are going to help our hearts to grow. And we realize what is important in our lives—our friends and our family. But it is our relationship with our Maker that is of utmost importance.*

You might think that was the end of Glenn's story. But as a true testament to his "never give up" attitude, Glenn continues to drive himself into the future—in a big way. He became the star of the Discovery Channel show, *The Undercover Billionaire*. In an interview with *Business Insider*, he shared he was doing the show because "Life is short and I don't want to breathe my last and have regrets." Wait, there's more! In 2020, Glenn launched Kind Lending. His website states, "After a sabbatical where he spent time with his family and visualized the next evolution of wholesale lending, industry leader Glenn Stearns is back and ready to unleash his inimitable vision, grit, and passion on a revolutionary venture." He's definitely back!

Am I glad to know Glenn? Yes! Am I grateful for the many significant lessons he has taught me? Absolutely! Do I expect that his Power of Persistence will pay off over the long term? I have no doubt!

Fishing buddies come in all sizes — me, Tom Chambers, and Glenn Stearns at Langara Island, BC.

## Never Underestimate the Power of Persistence

Be sure to get a copy of Glenn's book, *InteGRITy*, published by Forefront Books, and available through many book outlets including Amazon.

## CHAPTER TWENTY
# THE POWER OF GIVING BACK

Have you ever noticed that there are two kinds of people in the world? There are *givers* and there are *takers*. My personal view is that *takers* believe the world owes them something, maybe even everything. *Givers* believe that the world (through their hard work, education, and persistence) has given them so much that they owe something back. Their desire is to give back.

Now, I admit that it's easier for people to give when they're living in "plenty" and more difficult to give when they're living with "little." Financial hardship makes it difficult to think beyond one's immediate needs.

It's true that those with fewer resources can also give in other ways. But this chapter is about those people I know with plenty, who also give and why they do. The bottom line is that we can all find a way to make a difference in the world.

If you were to meet and talk with a cross-section of successful people, you would likely discover two things. First, most of them are grateful for the success they've achieved. They realize their success is partly hard work, but it's also partly being in the right place at the right time. Second, many of them want to give back. They want to help build better communities and a better world.

## 20. The Power of Giving Back

These people have different and highly personal ways of expressing their philanthropic desires. They might create a foundation or give to causes that seek to cure illnesses. Perhaps they feed the hungry or help build facilities that further education. They may give to some organizations that have helped them in the past—boys and girls clubs or the Salvation Army. They might even give to a homeless shelter that provided refuge for their mothers and their siblings in a time of great pain and enormous need. Of course, you don't need lots of disposable cash to give in big ways. You can still serve meals to the homeless or become a scout leader. Many wealthy donors add to their financial donations by giving their time as well.

The fact is that most of these people weren't born rich. Many entrepreneurs I know started with nothing. They were part of what we know as the "99%." But through hard work, perseverance, the guidance of mentors, and in many cases, faith, they overcame poverty, a lack of education, or other obstacles they faced to rise to extraordinary success.

Remember the Horatio Alger Award created by Norman Vincent Peale? You wouldn't believe the stories of the people who've won this award. They're children of the unschooled, of drug addicts, of oppressed minority groups. Many had limited formal education. Yet they turned their lives around, and then they gave to others.

Bill Gates of Microsoft may not have been the child of drug addicts, but he wasn't highly educated, either. He's been called "Harvard's most successful dropout." Yet he amassed one of the largest fortunes in American history—and now his goal is to give most of it away.

## 20. The Power of Giving Back

What about Bernie Marcus, who founded Home Depot along with Arthur Blank? Now retired, he devotes his time and energy to a foundation with an outreach that circles the globe. As a gift to Atlanta, the city that gave him his start, he built the now-famous Georgia Aquarium. Countless schoolchildren and families can enjoy this amazing destination.

It's true that money has the power to enrich and change lives. It doesn't matter how much money someone makes. What matters is that we all share . . . that we give to the needs of others.

I believe that there are basic principles that underlie the concept of giving.

## My Basic Principles of Giving

**First**: *Giving isn't based on your wealth.* It's based on your desire to help others. It's your *attitude*, not the *amount you give*, that matters.

**Second**: *Something is better than nothing.* You don't have to start big. Giving canned goods to "Stamp-Out Hunger," the food drive sponsored by the National Association of Letter Carriers, is a good start. Your donation of clothes to Goodwill or a homeless shelter means more to them than you will ever know.

**Third**: *Be happy—even cheerful—about what you're giving.* Isn't that what the Bible tells us? Don't look at what you're losing, consider what others are gaining. When you think about the good you're doing for others, it will make you happy.

## 20. The Power of Giving Back

To summarize: Make all you can. Save all you can. And give all you can.

Foster Friess, me, Ted Purdy, and Chris Grogan — four good men, one great day, dove hunting in Arizona.

### Foster Friess

One of my closest friends was Foster Friess, a native of the small town of Rice Lake, Wisconsin. We were so connected that we'd talk to each other at least once a week, and I valued his counsel and his friendship.

Foster was a first-generation college graduate. His mother dropped out of school in the eighth grade to pick cotton in order to save the family farm in Texas. His father dealt in cattle and horses. But Foster graduated from high school as valedictorian, class president, student council president, and captain of the basketball, track, golf, and baseball teams. At the University of Wisconsin, he earned a degree in business administration, served as president of his fraternity, was named one of the "ten most outstanding senior men," and won the heart of "Badger Beauty" and

## 20. The Power of Giving Back

Chi Omega president Lynnette Estes, whom he married in 1962. Two sons, two daughters, and fifteen grandchildren followed.

In 1974, after serving our nation as both an infantry platoon leader and an intelligence officer, Foster and his wife launched the investment management firm, Friess Associates, LLC. During the 1990s, the firm's flagship investment fund, the Brandywine Fund, averaged 20 percent annual gains, making Foster and Lynn a very wealthy couple. *Forbes* magazine named it one of the decade's top mutual funds, and CNBC dubbed Foster one of the "century's great investors." Foster credits much of his success to his team-building abilities, but he doesn't keep all the money he's made for himself.

Foster and Lynn are known for their donations and generosity to their local communities. They provided Foster's hometown school, Rice Lake High School, with a $3.7 million complex that included football, baseball, softball, and track fields. In 2016, Foster offered a matching grant to "Rachel's Challenge," a nonprofit organization started in the name of Rachel Scott, the first victim of the Columbine High School massacre. The purpose of the organization is to create a chain reaction of kindness to end bullying and drug abuse. In the last three years, the organization has averted seven school shootings and more than 500 suicides.

After the Parkland shooting in 2018, Foster established a $2.5 million matching grant for the "Return to Civility Fund" through the National Christian Foundation. The fund develops programs to improve school safety, foster youth mentoring, and promote a return to civility in the schools.

## 20. The Power of Giving Back

In addition, the Friess Family Foundation has provided millions of dollars of aid in response to numerous global natural disasters, including victims of the 2004 Indonesian tsunami, Hurricane Katrina, and the 2010 Haiti earthquake.

Foster gave more than anyone I've ever met, and he has the trophies to prove it. In 1999, the "Champ" himself awarded him the Muhammad Ali Humanitarian Award. In 2000, at the National Charity Awards Dinner in Washington, D.C., Foster was named the "Humanitarian of the Year," following in the footsteps of Coretta Scott King, Bob Hope, President George H.W. Bush, and Lady Bird Johnson.

Foster could be quite creative in giving. To commemorate his 70th birthday, he invited about 120 couples to write a description of a favorite charity that best reflected the values of his favorite quote from Galatians: "Carry each other's burdens, and in this way, you will fulfill the law of Christ." He said he'd make out a check for $70,000 to his favorite description and ten checks for $7,000 each to the runners-up. Then he gave everyone an envelope. When the time came to announce the winning charity, Foster had everyone open their envelope. The winner was to shout, "I got it!" After opening their envelopes, everyone in the room shouted, "I got it!" Foster had surprised his guests by writing $70,000 checks to all of their charities. It worked out to almost $8 million!

When he unselfishly gave to charity, Foster would say something like, "If this were my money, you wouldn't get a penny, but since it's all God's money, I just love giving it away." I was happy to present my $70,000 check to one of my favorite charities, the Joe Foss Institute. Wouldn't it be great if stories like this would make the news more often?

## 20. The Power of Giving Back

**Awarding Foster Friess the "Grand Dufus" award along with his personal copy of Fishing for Dummies at the 2008 El Dorado Fishing Trip in British Columbia, Canada.**

But Foster had another side to him that makes me smile and even laugh. You see, he's one of those people who could mess up a two-car parade. He could be a klutz. Let me explain. I love to give out trophies on my hunting and fishing trips. At my ranch each year, I also give an award for "top hand" and one to the winner of mounted shooting, shooting clays, and horseshoes events. But there's another award I give to the individual who does the most brainless or funny deed. The trophy is appropriately called the "Grand Dufus" award. I've lost count of how many of these awards Foster has garnered over the years. I've included a picture of him receiving his 2008 "Grand Dufus" award. Being Foster, he found a way to get back at me after my first edition of

## 20. The Power of Giving Back

*The Master Plan* came out. He told everyone he saw that my book was being republished as "fire log" material!

In 2018, Foster formed "Foster's Outriders." Just as cattle outriders keep the herd together and on the right path, the organization's members are hardworking Americans who try to keep our country on the right path. Foster grew up believing that all people were created equal—despite our differences. His organization offers scholarships to people entering the trades, provides free access to civics education and programs, and gives Good Neighbor grants to people and organizations that have made a difference in their community. Working with Democrats, Republicans, and Independents, the foundation strives to unite Americans from all backgrounds around issues we can all agree on.

I'm sad to say that my good friend Foster Friess passed away on May 27, 2021. But the members of Foster's Outriders continue working with Americans of all backgrounds to keep America on the right trail.

**There is something about the outside of a horse that is good for the inside of a man—mounted shooting at Bell Cross Ranch.**

20. The Power of Giving Back

**When Arizona turns up the heat, Montana is where I cool down and loosen the reins.**

# 20. The Power of Giving Back

## Jerry Moyes

Giving back does not always mean writing a check to your favorite cause. It can mean empowering other people to become successful—through mentoring them, investing your time with them, or even providing a loan to help them reach for their dreams.

One of my good friends in business is a man named Jerry Moyes. I refer to Jerry as the "Number One Truck Driver in America" because he started with one truck and built his company, Swift Transportation, into one of the largest trucking companies in the nation. In 2006, Jerry owned only 40 percent of the stock in the publicly traded Swift, and he was voted out as Chairman and CEO by the board of directors.

**Jerry Moyes, founder of Swift Transportation, doing what he does best – showing up and hauling big.**

## 20. The Power of Giving Back

But you can't stop a man like Jerry that easily. He worked diligently and meticulously to buy back the company he had started. He accomplished his goal and took the company private in 2008. When Jerry once again took Swift public in 2011, he was careful to keep 67 percent of the voting stock.

In 2017, Swift merged with Knight Transportation and Jerry was the major stockholder of this company, which is now the largest common carrier in the U.S. He is ranked on the *Forbes* list as one of the wealthiest businessmen in the U.S. Jerry's talent is to go from billionaire, to broke, to billionaire—and still maintain his unpretentious character.

Jerry has never forgotten how he started. He always remembers those who helped him and finds ways to pay them back. One case involved a man named Lon Emerson. In fact, Lon introduced me to Jerry, who then became an investor in many of our projects.

I recall meeting up with Jerry one day to show him a possible investment called Rio Verde 832. Lon also happened to be there. He'd helped Jerry get started in the trucking business. Lon was a representative of a large cotton marketing company and had given Jerry some of his very first freight hauls. Jerry had never forgotten that Lon was an instrumental player in building his business.

That day Jerry said, "You know, Mike, I'm going to take 15 percent of this investment and put $200,000 of it in Lon's name. Of course, he needs to get approval from his boss and board of directors, but this is what I want to do."

Turning to Lon, he explained, "Lon, this is a loan. The deal is, I want my $200,000 back and seven percent interest. But you can keep the profits on the investments."

## 20. The Power of Giving Back

After about a year, we sold half of it. I told Jerry I had checks to deliver. He replied, "That's great. Figure out Lon's cut, but remember, I get $200,000 back—plus interest."

The three of us met in Jerry's office. I handed Jerry his check and said, "Here's your $200,000 plus the interest Lon owes you."

Next, I turned to Lon. "Lon, the rest of this is yours." I handed him the check. When Lon looked at it, he couldn't speak. The check was for more than $600,000. Lon was so overcome with emotion he had to leave the room. Jerry was so pleased!

A few months later, we sold the other half of Rio Verde 832, and Lon's share was around $400,000. Between these two sales, Lon had made about a million dollars—thanks to the generosity of Jerry Moyes.

A couple of months later, Lon came to see me. Now, you have to understand, Lon is fairly large in stature and can look a bit intimidating. When I met him in the conference room, he came after me, saying, "I'm going to kiss you. I'm telling you, I'm just going to kiss you" and chased me around the conference table. Finally, I convinced him it was Jerry Moyes he needed to kiss, not me.

Then Lon said, "I want to show you what I've done. First, I have a check here made out to my church. I'm going to use some of the money to help build a couple of churches in Hungary. Also, I met with my accountant, and we've set aside certain funds for these earnings. Next, I bought a car for each of my three kids. And I sent money to my brother and sister so they could each buy themselves a car. Plus, I've already written a check to cover my taxes."

## 20. The Power of Giving Back

That's not all. Lon and his wife had lived most of their married life in a simple house that was valued at less than $100,000. Now he could treat his wife to a new home—though not the most luxurious house they could afford because Lon is careful with money and has his priorities in order. Since that day, Lon Emerson has invested his own money in our partnerships.

With that one deal, Jerry Moyes had completely changed one family's whole financial outlook. It was not an isolated instance either. Jerry has also made investments with El Dorado for three other individuals in positions similar to Lon's and with great results! One particular investment has already returned over six-fold Jerry's original investment and still has a portion of the property remaining for future sales.

Jerry shares his success through his giving heart. People who don't understand giving don't understand how much fun it is to make a powerful impact on the lives of others.

**Two Indiana Boys, a Cowboy and a Trucker; Vice President Mike Pence, me, Jerry Moyes and Vice President Dan Quayle.**

SUCCE$$ DEMANDS A MASTER PLAN

## 20. The Power of Giving Back

### Reba McEntire

I have the pleasure of calling Reba McEntire my friend. She comes up to my ranch in Montana every summer where we compete on horseback and mounted shooting. Reba usually wins the contest. She often wins the sporting clay shooting contests too. She's a very tough competitor.

Other people often ask me what she's really like. It's true that she's famous, but she still treats everyone as if they're her best friends. If I had one word to describe Reba McEntire, it would definitely be "humble." Look up the definition of humble in Merriam-Webster's Dictionary. You will find words like "down-to-earth, modest, unassuming, and unpretentious." That's Reba.

**Sheila, Rex Linn, Reba McEntire and me; another beautiful day at the ranch with great friends.**

Not only is Reba humble, she's also a tremendous giver. In 1992, she opened Reba's Ranch House in Denison, Texas. Since then, she's been putting on concerts, golf and fishing tournaments, and parades, all to raise money for the facility.

## 20. The Power of Giving Back

People often have to travel miles to spend time with a family member at a hospital in North Texas or South Oklahoma. Reba's Ranch House provides a place where they can sleep and get a home-cooked meal during stressful times.

Reba is an active supporter of many charities, including Habitat for Humanity® and Feeding America®, and she also inspires others to give more. Her warmth and hospitality make everyone present pull out their wallets. For the past fifteen years, Reba has served as the emcee of Celebrity Fight Night in Phoenix. It's an annual, star-studded charity event that has provided about $90 million to a number of charities, especially the Barrow Neurological Foundation.

**Sheila, Red Steagall, Reba McEntire, and me at Phoenix's Celebrity Fight Night — an amazing event that Reba has proudly hosted since the early 2000s.**

When Reba received the Andrea Bocelli Foundation Humanitarian Award at the twentieth annual Celebrity Fight Night event in Italy, she described her charitable work by saying, "To know that you can lend a hand and make someone's life a little better brings you back up to realize

## 20. The Power of Giving Back

why you are on this earth in the first place, and that's learning how you can grow as a better person by giving and loving."

### Boysie Bollinger

I need to bring up Boysie Bollinger again. If you recall, he grew up in his dad's shipyard and is now Chairman and Chief Executive Officer of Bollinger Shipyards, a full-service marine construction and ship repair company headquartered in Lockport, Louisiana, with ten divisions in Louisiana and another one in Texas.

**Dave Garcia, Shon Craig, Alex Ryan, me, Budd Florkiewicz, Boysie Bollinger, Chris Breed and Wes Bates. Good hunt, better wine, best company!**

But Boysie is involved far beyond the shipyard! He gives back in so many ways. His father taught him that he had to give back, not just in resources, but in time and in service. He encouraged all his kids to be involved in service, as well as in careers. "It made a huge difference in my life," Boysie says. "Number one, I think it developed my leadership skills. I've been involved with probably thirty to forty organizations,

## 20. The Power of Giving Back

all of which I've chaired." He says he goes in without an objective, except to do good for the group.

Boysie serves on the boards of many groups and devotes considerable time to professional and civic organizations. He serves on more boards and has received more awards than about anyone I know. Louisiana Public Broadcasting once named him a "Louisiana Legend." His "trophy room" is bursting with well-deserved awards!

But his greatest single achievement is his support of the National World War II Museum in New Orleans. He believes that the "greatest generation," referred to in Tom Brokaw's bestselling book with that title, deserves to be honored this way. He's the museum's largest contributor and funded the Bollinger Canopy of Peace, an iconic structure that spans the Museum's campus and visually unifies its various buildings as a symbol of hope, following the American experience in World War II. An added benefit? It's also a stunning addition to the New Orleans skyline.

This museum should definitely be on your bucket list. When Boysie talks about it, he says, "The one thing that I'm really hoping is that the museum continues to tell the story for our young people, so they don't lose sight of the price that has been paid by those who've gone before us and those that have fought for our freedoms. It's so easy for us to take it for granted."

Boysie Bollinger is a remarkable example of a simple truth: "When your ship comes in and you are financially empowered, it's your responsibility to send other ships back on the seas, to deliver boundless treasures to other people

# 20. The Power of Giving Back

and other significant causes." Giving back has long been his primary vision, and he's been doing it for decades.

## Why I Love to Give

I suppose I could have retired a few years ago, but then I wouldn't be following John Wesley's advice that I heard so many years ago. In his famous sermon called "The Use of Money," he said that it involves three basic principles: "Earn all you can, save all you can, and give all you can."

I learned about the importance of giving at an early age, from my parents and from other family members. My mother's brother was a farmer in New Mexico. People who knew him thought he must be one of the richest men in the state. Every time he made any money, he gave it away. Meanwhile, he always drove an old car and wore shoes or clothes that were in poor shape. It didn't matter. He loved people, and in many respects, it was his giving that made him rich. He was one of the happiest people I ever met. He lived to be about 90 years old—giving to others until the end.

## Caring for My Investors

Many of my investors in El Dorado have been partnering with me since the company's beginning in 1987. Because many of them were in their fifties and sixties at the time, a good number have passed away over the years. Every time I hear of health problems with one of my investors, my heart goes out to them and their families. After thirty or more years, these people and their families have become *my* family.

## 20. The Power of Giving Back

When an investor passes away, I work hard to remain involved with their surviving widow and family. In many cases, the widow continues to be an El Dorado investor as well as the children who don't stop investing with us. To this day, the grandchildren of some of my original investors remain partners—third generation partners!

To honor the wonderful investors we've lost, Sheila and I host an annual Valentine's Day party for those widows who are still with us. We never want them to be alone or lonely on that day, and we want to let them know they have someone who loves them. Several have been blessed by finding another partner to share in their lives, but they still want to be included in the party. Naturally, we invite them to continue to attend and bring their new spouses! Usually, we host around thirty-five widows each year. It's a wonderful event.

We typically have a top-notch speaker, good music, good food, and great company. We make sure that every special guest goes home with flowers, chocolates, and a special surprise each year—a gift certificate for Victoria's Secret! Yes, the ladies get a good chuckle and some joy out of that. It makes them feel younger, even though most of them give the gift certificates to their granddaughters! Some widows have been coming every year since we initiated this dinner more than thirty years ago.

## 20. The Power of Giving Back

A truly special Valentine's Dinner spent with two incredible women — Yvonne Fedderson and Sara O'Meara. What a joy and an honor to share the evening with such inspiring hearts.

### The Pinnacle Forum

Personally, I enjoy giving in ways that don't always involve money. I was inspired, along with five others, to start an organization in Phoenix called the Pinnacle Forum. The concept is to bring together people of influence in the community to discuss life's most important ethical principles. Note that I said people of "influence," and not people of "affluence." I'm talking about leaders, whether they're in business, agriculture, education, or politics. Having money is not the key concern.

The Pinnacle Forum consists of groups of eight to twelve peers who meet regularly in a confidential setting, where we encourage and support each other in learning how to live life most effectively. Partners in the forums grow personally and professionally, discover their passions, and become more sensitive about how best to contribute to the greater good. They share experiences, opportunities, and needs, and they support and motivate one another—with the ultimate vision of cultural transformation.

I was joined by Jerry Colangelo, Dave Hall, Dave Caven, John Lang, and Merrill Oster to start the first group in Phoenix. Merrill and I had the desire to take the program nationally, and I am delighted to report that about 100 forums are now being held in forty-four cities across the country. For me, Pinnacle Forum is a commitment of my time, and I believe that time can be as purposeful a way to give back as money. Yes, I have contributed dollars, but the most valuable contribution is time given.

## Athletes in Action

I've been involved with Athletes in Action for almost twenty years. It's a ministry of Campus Crusade for Christ International, a global community that joins with college, professional, and top amateur athletes and coaches to reach the lives of millions through sports. Their goal is to help coaches and athletes grow "physically, mentally, and spiritually," both on and off the field.

Each year, this great organization presents the Bart Starr Award to the NFL player who clearly demonstrates leadership on the field, in the community, and at home. It's presented at a special Super Bowl breakfast typically held on the morning prior to the Super Bowl game. The award is voted on by NFL players—peers are casting their vote for the player they believe is most distinguished in exemplary leadership. It's a simple example of a way to give that touches lives. It's about the "charity of caring."

## 20. The Power of Giving Back

### Other People's Passions

One of the joys of giving for me, personally, is to give to other people's passions. Most people have a passion for something. It may be for helping out an animal shelter, or supporting abused children, or assisting wounded warriors—service men and women who return home with injuries that have severely altered their lives. If you help people with their passions, then they'll help you with your passion. It's one way of making good on Zig Ziglar's idea: "You can have everything in life you want, if you will just help enough other people get what they want."

Sometimes, I get a little too eager to share my passions with my friends, according to a few of them. Foster Friess once told me he'd sent out applications to replace me as his friend. Others have told me they can't *afford* to be my friend any longer. I guess I had one too many fundraisers this past year!

Giving back is the key to any Master Plan, not to mention the obvious benefits. If you're not actively giving back as part of your plan, you're missing out on one of the true joys of life.

# CHAPTER TWENTY-ONE
# THE POWER OF MENTORING

Me with my trusted partner and President of El Dorado Holdings, Chris Grogan, riding the range and checking cows at Bell Cross Ranch.

You're probably wondering why an old guy like me (I turned eighty in 2024) hasn't retired yet. The fact is that I love what I do. I've always mixed my business with pleasure. It's how I get to know people, especially my investors. While I'm out fishing, hunting, or riding horses with people I know, I'm connecting, building trust, and networking. Who would want to give that up?

## 21. The Power of Mentoring

I'm also realistic. The day will come when I'll have to ride into the sunset, but first I need to take care of what I've left behind—my business, my family, my investors, my charities, and my employees (whom I think of as partners in my business). I want them to survive for a good long time after I leave El Dorado Holdings.

I like to think of it this way: I gave birth to the business; now I need someone to take it to the next level. I believe . . . I know . . . I've found the right person. Chris Grogan is the man who's destined to lead El Dorado Holdings into the future. Let me tell you a little about him. Then I'll let him speak for himself.

Chris Grogan was born and raised in Phoenix. His father was in the real estate business and eventually settled in Arizona. I never did business with Chris's dad, but we ran in the same circles, so I got to know him. One day, Chris's father told me I should meet with his son, although he didn't tell me a lot about him. I'll let Chris take it from here.

**Me and Chris Grogan, El Dorado Holdings President –
the best lessons stick when you're in it together.**

## Chris Grogan

*As Mike mentioned, I kind of grew up in the real estate business. After graduating college in Massachusetts, I returned to Arizona in late 2006. It was a year before the last big recession and businesses were wary. It was hard for me to find work, so I did odd jobs in construction and worked for a year as an unpaid intern for Carlson Real Estate. Then I moved into the brokerage world at CB Richard Ellis and spent five years there. About a month after I started, the market crashed.*

*This may sound funny, but it couldn't have worked out better for me. It was the middle-management people with two houses and a boat who stressed out. You see, when everything is going well, realtors tend to focus only on advertising and marketing themselves. Some of them had already created bad habits, and a good market can cover a lot of mistakes. But I believe the market is the market. No matter how good you think you are, you aren't negotiating or selling in a bad market. Recognizing that is a huge part of understanding how to be a good real estate professional. Many of the middle people above me lost money and had to get other jobs.*

*I was young, had no money, and was still eating ramen noodles. It was the best time for someone like me to learn real estate—what the actual problems are and how to solve them, what people are looking for, and how to add value to people's businesses. The crash actually created a vacuum of talent in the real estate business. It was full of young, inexperienced people like me; retirement-ready, experienced professionals; and nothing in between. You could say I was in the right place at the right time.*

## 21. The Power of Mentoring

*And then my dad told me that Mike Ingram wanted to talk to me. I'll never forget the first time I met Mike at his office. Picture this: he and his staff are dressed to the nines, which is unusual where we live. It turns out they had a meeting with the governor. I suddenly figure Mike is expecting someone more experienced, someone in his mid-thirties or even forties. I think to myself, "What am I doing here?" I'm just a twenty-seven-year-old with a couple of flyers about properties. Mike looks at me and asks, "What are you doing at my table?" I give him a little spiel about my job at CB Richard Ellis. When I finish, he says, "Let me tell you a little about El Dorado." From that point on, it's just me listening.*

*After talking about the history of El Dorado, he said he'd sold everything he had to sell so far and hadn't bought any property since 2005. El Dorado had been in a holding pattern during the recession and Mike convinced his investors they needed to be patient. He also hadn't put together any partnerships with new investors for some time. Many of his partners, who'd been with him for over thirty years, had grown older and died, passing down their partnerships to their kids and grandkids. He told me he'd gone to eighteen funerals so far. Mike had a decision to make. Should he put new partnerships together or should he wind down his current partnerships and retire?*

*"I love what I do," Mike said, "and I love my investors dearly." But he didn't see himself reselling El Dorado Holdings to the sons and daughters of his original investors. Mike may be a brilliant salesman, but he's never felt comfortable using the latest technology. He felt he needed someone he could feel confident about, somebody who could talk to these younger*

## 21. The Power of Mentoring

*people and connect with them for him. We talked about these things for the better part of three months. I met some of his partners along the way and got to do some fun stuff, like trail rides and dinners with him. I guess you could say that Mike was vetting me to see how I'd respond to the business development side of El Dorado Holdings. Mike's business is unusual. It's a network of people who are like friends and family to him. His group of LLCs was a living, breathing thing, and he wanted to know how I'd react to them.*

*Mike offered me a job, but before I could make a decision, I needed to know that he was going to continue on with El Dorado for another ten or more years to make it worth my while. His answer was clear. "This is my life," he as much as said. "My partners are my friends. I travel with them, invest with them, and put together partnerships with them." If Mike retired, he wouldn't be able to donate to the many charities he and his partners support. The bottom line for Mike wasn't about the money; it was about the network, the people involved, the different charities, the entire ecosystem.*

*When I left CB Richard Ellis, I was on the verge of making much more money, and I left to work for Mike with a cut in pay. But the roof lifted for me, and I've never regretted my choice.*

*Mike put me to work right away, planning a lot of the special events he and Sheila had managed in the past—pheasant hunting in October, fishing trip in August, Montana trip in June and July, and the rodeo in December. My goal was to take their system, add on to it, and bring technology into the picture. All Mike and Sheila had to do was show up and enjoy themselves. Meanwhile, on the brokerage side, I'd look for new deals, value the deals, and see if we could sell or buy*

## 21. The Power of Mentoring

something. On the investor side, I'd meet with staff, hear from our engineers and planners, put the information together in a PowerPoint, and take it on the road, where I could explain it in simple terms to our investors. The idea was to make everything work more smoothly and efficiently.

From the time I started working for Mike, he was so inclusive and so open that I couldn't help but learn through osmosis. His mentorship was full-blown inclusivity and his willingness to answer all my questions. There was a time when he had ankle surgery, and I became his driver. As a result, I went to meetings that I might not have gone to otherwise. Afterwards, we'd debrief on the drive back.

I'll never forget the first time I met with Jerry Colangelo, a titan of industry, former owner of the Phoenix Suns and the Diamondbacks, four-time winner of the NBA Executive of the Year Award, and my idol. There I was, sitting in a corner of the room listening to Mike, Jerry, and several other businessmen discuss Douglas Ranch, the people around Phoenix, and the future of Arizona. I thought of a question, which reminded me of a joke, and I laughed. I didn't want them to think I was a total idiot, so I shut my mouth and continued to listen.

Later, when I got in the car, I asked Mike my question. He said, "Why didn't you ask that at the meeting?" I said I didn't know if it was my place. "You were in the room, weren't you?" Mike replied. I took that as a lesson to take my shot and ask my question whenever I'm in the room. Who cares if Jerry Colangelo thinks I'm an idiot? Maybe my question will spark a conversation or maybe they'll tell me not to worry about it. If nothing else, it'll show I'm not afraid to talk to them, to take

## 21. The Power of Mentoring

*the stage. And that's how Mike's mentorship works. It's in his actions. It's being part of the process.*

*There's one more reason I was drawn to Mike in the first place. He and I have very similar beliefs. We both have a Western spirit in us. Something about the cowboy and the code of the West attracted me to Mike and the beliefs he writes about in this book. It's the power of relationships. We're not doing anything in this world on our own. We're just stewards of other people's money. That really struck a chord with me.*

Now that you've heard from Chris, let me tell you what I see. Chris has all the natural abilities in the world. He's exceptionally smart, has a tremendous amount of people skills, and understands today's technology. He can research things in a matter of minutes. While I'm comfortable communicating with my friends and partners the old-fashioned way, Chris can connect with people using more modern techniques. He also has many natural instincts, which make him a natural leader. People love him.

I could see it was time to move out of the way so the company could continue to grow. As I mentioned earlier, I put our company together and got it started. Chris and some of the other young people coming on today can take it much further than I've done so far. What do I mean by getting out of the way? There are organizations out there that you can't be part of unless you possess the title. People always want to talk to the guy that's got the title. That's why I made Chris a partner and President of El Dorado Holdings. People also want to talk to the person who knows what's going on. In my day, it was Deb Bricker from the start. I was the salesperson,

## 21. The Power of Mentoring

but she was the glue who held things together. When she decides to retire someday, I'm sure Chris will find someone else to be his Deb.

From the start, Chris has been deeply involved with the company. He searches for new investment opportunities and markets the properties we already have. What's most important to me is that he has a great relationship with our investors. He's the one who'll give leadership to our company, not just for our kids and grandkids, but also for the investors we've brought in. It's his responsibility to make their investments continue to grow, and I'm confident that he'll lead El Dorado Holdings to an even greater future.

## CHAPTER TWENTY-TWO
# THE POWER OF FREEDOM

I love America! I love the freedom and opportunity our country offers to all of us. If you haven't noticed my personal bias by now, this is your reminder.

Overall, the world is a wonderful place, despite the wars that need to be ended, the suffering that begs to be healed, the illnesses that demand cures, and the spiritual needs that pray to be addressed. Nations around the world offer opportunities for people of all races, creeds, and socioeconomic backgrounds to create better lives for themselves. But none compare, I believe, with the United States of America.

My cloth envelope business card holder — because my love for America is stitched into every detail.

## 22. The Power of Freedom

When I meet new business prospects and potential partners, I make it known that I love our country, that I'm a patriot, and that I'm not ashamed of that fact. That's why I enclose my business cards in small envelopes that bear a picture of the Stars and Stripes. When I hand my cards out, it helps people remember our flag in a positive way.

I've decided to add an element for those times when I want to make an extra impression. Maybe it's because of my love for the TV series, *The Lone Ranger,* from my youth or because of my marketing background. If you're old enough, you may recall the Lone Ranger always left a silver bullet behind. It was his calling card. The lines I remember were, "Who was that masked man?" and the answer, "I don't know, but he left a silver bullet." They were a symbol of justice and a reminder that life, like silver, has value and is not to be wasted or thrown away. So, I've designed a silver bullet (not real silver) engraved with my name and business.

Remember, I basically started with nothing. My dad died when I was thirteen years old, and I worked alongside my mom to keep our small thirty-four-unit New Mexico motel from foreclosure. Years later, I had a successful business that was on the edge of failure, and I couldn't find a bank that would loan me a dime, so I sold everything for pennies on the dollar. I moved to Arizona in a rented U-Haul truck and rebuilt my life with my wife, Sheila, at my side.

That's why I love the United States of America. What makes our nation so special is the opportunity it offers to everyone, regardless of the situations in which we were born. And what turns those opportunities into positive realities are the values we hold close to our hearts. I've

## 22. The Power of Freedom

shared my thoughts on many of those values in the pages of this book: integrity, teamwork, trust, loyalty, forgiveness, and persistence, among others.

Now I'm inspired to do my part to help make America a better nation—and our world a better place for all—by passing on these values to the next generation. I believe that all who live in a free society, no matter where in the world, have a responsibility to do everything we can to promote and protect our values. Paul Harvey, the late, great news commentator, put it this way: "For me, success is to leave the woodpile a little higher than I found it."

Unless you grew up "rural," you may not know what this expression means. In the old days, people who were traveling across the country would come across unoccupied cabins that were open to visitors. The owners would leave the doors unlocked so that weary travelers could find rest and shelter. There would usually be a stack of wood outside so that the travelers could build a warm fire. In those days, no considerate traveler would ever burn all the wood without chopping more and replacing the logs and kindling they'd taken from the woodpile.

That's what we must do as a society. That's what we need to do as a country. We have to leave the woodpile just a little higher than it was when we inherited it. If we don't, our kids, our grandkids, and generations coming after them are going to be faced with major problems. We're burning the wood now and we're burning it at an unbelievable rate.

Many people are concerned about leaving the woodpile higher than they found it. Our men and women of the armed services are doing it. Not only are they defending our

## 22. The Power of Freedom

freedoms, but also, they contribute to humanitarian causes in the lands they defend.

The servicemen and servicewomen of today's military have joined the countless Americans who fought in the Revolutionary War and the wars that followed: the Civil War, World War I, World War II, the Korean War, the Vietnam War, and the War on Terrorism. Those heroes paid a tremendous price. Their monumental sacrifice has defended one of the greatest democracies ever formed—against enemies both foreign and domestic.

In my travels I've encountered many active servicemen, servicewomen and veterans. Some have given me what is called a "challenge coin." It's a part of military tradition and a sign of fellowship and solidarity. I've always been honored to receive them. Recently, I selected a challenge coin of my own to share with others. One side of the coin states, "Land of the Free Because of the Brave." On the other side, it says, "Honoring Those who Protect our Freedom. We Stand for The Flag."

### Joe Foss

Not everyone in our country is aware of the history of our Constitution and the Bill of Rights. I want to fight that trend. That's why I got involved with the Joe Foss Institute. This nonprofit organization offers free programs that teach students about the importance of America's freedoms and encourage them to be involved in active citizenship.

I met Joe many years ago. In my mind, he was bigger than life, a real-world John Wayne. He was born and raised on a farm in South Dakota. When World War II broke out,

## 22. The Power of Freedom

Joe enlisted. He became one of the most decorated airmen in the war, shooting down twenty-six Japanese warplanes. For that, he was awarded the Congressional Medal of Honor—the highest award given for military valor.

When the Korean War began, Joe decided he wanted to serve again. He was told he was too old and already a hero, so he didn't need to serve again. Joe disagreed, so he joined the Air Force. He eventually retired from military life as both a general in the Air Force and a captain in the Marines. Joe had a powerful perspective with his passion to serve his country. He simply said, "Those of us who lived have to represent those who didn't make it."

After his return to South Dakota, he was elected governor and finished out both terms in office. Then he became Commissioner of the American Football League (AFL), a new league created to take on the supremacy of the NFL. Joe challenged the legendary Pete Rozelle to set up a game pitting the AFL's championship team against the NFL's. Pete finally yielded to the idea, believing that the two leagues weren't anywhere close to the same level. But in the third year, Joe's AFL team, the New York Jets, led by quarterback Joe Namath, won the game. And that, football fans, led to the creation of the Super Bowl and the merger of the NFL with the AFL.

Joe was witty, smart, incisive, and decisive—four great qualities in any individual. He told me that when he was Governor of South Dakota and later Commissioner of the AFL, people would come to him and say, "We have a problem." Joe would stop them in their tracks and ask, "Is this problem life threatening to me or to one of my family

## 22. The Power of Freedom

members?" They would answer, "Well, no, but we have a problem." He would respond, "No sir, you don't. I know what a problem is. I've been shot down behind enemy lines three times, and I have stared down the barrel of a gun in enemy hands. I know what a problem is. What you are talking about is a situation that has to be dealt with. It is not a problem."

Maybe the one thing Joe will be most remembered for is the Joe Foss Institute, which he co-founded with his wife, Didi. Their basic idea was to educate the youth of our nation about the principles of freedom. Joe believed Ronald Reagan had it right when he said we were just one generation away from losing our democracy. Reagan said that kids just don't understand it. He added they couldn't pick it up through osmosis or heredity. It was important to educate the next generation about the price that's been paid for the freedoms we all enjoy today.

Joe had a brilliant concept. To enlist veterans—he called them VIPs or Veterans Inspiring Patriotism—to help educate young people about our freedoms. Veterans would share personal stories in classrooms and to youth organizations, delivering educational materials that focused on the history of our constitutional republic: the Declaration of Independence, the Constitution, the Bill of Rights, and the U.S. flag. They talked about the price they—and their comrades who never returned from the battlefield—paid to defend freedom.

The Institute initiated a new program called E-Citizenship. It's a collaborative effort with educators around the country. The objective was to develop a lesson

## 22. The Power of Freedom

plan that can easily be implemented at no cost to the school district. The materials were also free. The Institute was going state by state, asking each to enact legislation requiring high school students to pass the same test that every immigrant must pass for citizenship in the United States.

In 2019, the Joe Foss Institute merged with Arizona State University's Center for American Civics to join forces to continue to expand civic education in schools nationwide.

The Joe Foss Institute is important to me because my freedom is important to me. I'm very much a patriot. I grew up saying the Pledge of Allegiance in school every day and am proud of it. I'm sorry that our pledge is not always required. I'm pleased, however, to see that so many Americans have "Support our Troops" ribbons on their cars. I've never served in the armed services, but I want to honor those who have sacrificed so much. I'm afraid that bravery, valor, and patriotism are underrated.

Every time I see a young serviceman or woman who is missing a leg, or an arm, or an eye, I think that a Purple Heart is nowhere near enough of a thank you for what they've given for the cause of freedom. I'd like to suggest that if you hire people or can influence hiring policies in your organization, you consider making a place in your heart and on your team for a returning veteran.

I know you've heard it before, but with freedom comes responsibility. I believe my responsibility is to leave the woodpile a little higher than I found it. That means I have to do everything possible to preserve and protect our freedoms by passing the values that shaped America onto the next generation. Please join me.

## 22. The Power of Freedom

**Astronaut Wally Schirra, me and my good friend and idol, Governor Joe Foss, dove hunting on some of our Maricopa, AZ property.**

# EPILOGUE:
# EL DORADO HOLDINGS TODAY

Since 1987, El Dorado Holdings has managed more than 110 successful real estate partnerships totaling over 83,000 acres. We've been responsible for the entitlement or development of over 50,000 lots and 2,000 acres of commercial and industrial properties. Those statistics come directly from our website, and I thought this might be a good time to give you a picture of all we've accomplished and where we're headed today. Here's a taste of what we've already accomplished:

### Rancho El Dorado – Maricopa, Arizona

This property, of course, is close to my heart. It was my first master-planned community and Maricopa's flagship property. I've already explained how this property, located in the heart of Maricopa, came about. I have to admit I'm proud of it. Against all odds, we took a piece of desert land and turned it into a beautiful home for thousands of people. We gave it the western feel of the original El Dorado Ranch and combined it with the agricultural history of the area. It has loads of amenities, including a community center with fitness facilities, two pools, playgrounds, a splash pad, as well as basketball and tennis courts. What more could you ask for?

Epilogue: El Dorado Holdings Today

## The Lakes at Rancho El Dorado – Maricopa, Arizona

This spectacular master-planned community offers an attractive option within the Rancho El Dorado Community, featuring stunning views and lovely lakes. Besides public schools and beautiful homes in a range of sizes, residents can enjoy parks, playgrounds, nature trails, and bike paths. It's the perfect place for an active family to grow up in.

## The Duke at Rancho El Dorado Golf Course – Maricopa, Arizona

The centerpiece of Rancho El Dorado, this golf course with its expansive fairways will remind you of the wide-open spaces of the Old West. Perfect for both the novice and the experienced golfer looking for a challenge, The Duke consistently ranks as one of the best courses in Arizona.

## Shamrock Estates – Gilbert, Arizona

In the early 2000s, El Dorado Holdings joined with Shamrock Foods and Taylor Morrison to develop a former dairy farm into a 582-acre community with 821 lots and about 25 acres of commercial property. Today, Shamrock Estates is home to many residents and retailers. It's also the residence of the Freedom Campus of the Chandler Traditional Academy, an early childhood school.

## El Dorado Tech Center and El Dorado Lakes – Gilbert, Arizona

This beautifully designed 438-acre master-planned development began in the early 1990s. The 108-acre technology park includes a large high-tech back office, as well as flex space for the growing employment base in the area. The adjacent El Dorado Lakes golf community consists of 500 single-family lots, a championship 18-hole golf club, and plenty of lifestyle amenities.

## Fox Crossing – Chandler, Arizona

Developed in late 1997 and early 1998, Fox Crossing was one of the first joint ventures in Arizona. El Dorado Holdings put together a joint development agreement with Capital Pacific Holdings and a number of home building companies for a 240-acre development with 787 lots. As a result, it's a diverse urban neighborhood with many amenities and picturesque lakes that add to its beauty.

## Springfield Community and Golf Resort – Chandler, Arizona

Springfield is an adult, gated retirement community that we entitled and developed in the mid-1990s. Our master plan included a 95-acre golf course surrounded by about 745 affordable, single-level homes for 55-plus seniors. This active community has lots of amenities, including pools, a recreation center, a fitness center, and sports courts. To add to the amenities, El Dorado Holdings also developed an additional 5 acres for a retail center.

## Circle Cross Ranch – San Tan Valley, Arizona

This planned community is a great place for families of all ages. Its walking paths and trails connect residents to a variety of parks and to lots where kids can play while their

# Epilogue: El Dorado Holdings Today

parents supervise them from shaded benches. The grassy open areas in the parks are perfect for playing Frisbee or soccer and holding neighborly picnics.

## Foothills Gateway – Phoenix, Arizona

El Dorado Holdings doesn't just develop land for homes. We believe in developing Arizona. Sometimes that means offering land for commercial development to provide jobs and amenities for our communities. In 1994, we acquired 27.8 acres along Interstate 10 and Chandler Road. We added improvements to the site, including underground infrastructure, water, sewer, utilities, grading, and paving. The site was developed for several commercial chains, including Holiday Inn Express, La Quinta Inn & Suites, Cracker Barrel Old Country Store, and Chevron.

As you can see, El Dorado Holdings has done a lot to improve life for people living in the areas surrounding Phoenix. And we're not finished yet. We're looking forward to a rich future with all the new folks moving to our part of the country. Besides starting our work on building a beautiful master-planned community at Floreo, we have bought a new area called Merrill Ranch with some of the money we made from the sale of Douglas Ranch to the Howard Hughes Corporation.

## Merrill Ranch – Florence, Arizona
## Now Known as Montanero

In 2023, a time when the economy caused land deals to come to a halt, El Dorado Holdings purchased 4,150 acres of vacant land within the town of Florence, Arizona.

## Epilogue: El Dorado Holdings Today

The site is made up of about 14,000 planned lots zoned for residences and 900 acres zoned for commercial use. Because of the downturn in the economy, we got a good deal on the purchase. During the bad times is the best time to buy. You still have to do your due diligence, and make sure you research and understand the assets and the property. But if you're smart, you'll realize your profits in the good times.

The large, up-and-coming, dynamic town of Florence has been around for a long time. The town has a lot of vision and will provide water and sewer services for the new community. Florence was looking for a partner to join in developing this vision, and we are fortunate to be that partner. The area already has a hospital, retail stores, and a school district, as well as plenty of water.

We always go into new towns by trying to understand their vision, what they've accomplished so far, and what they hope to accomplish. Then we try to fit into their vision, to create a "win-win" for everyone. That way we're not fighting an uphill battle. It's the only way to go. The town of Florence has some very talented leaders, so we're looking forward to another great marriage.

### Homes for Rent Communities

Until about three years ago, we were interested only in land development, nothing higher than the curb. But that doesn't work well in some income-producing properties, like office rentals, office buildings, or rental properties such as multifamily apartments. We were seeing people who wanted to rent but didn't want to live in an apartment. They didn't want their neighbors next to or on top of them.

## Epilogue: El Dorado Holdings Today

Instead, they wanted backyards and barbecues and a place for a dog. They also didn't want to buy or couldn't afford to. At the same time, they didn't want to fix broken toilets or repair lights. They didn't want to call a plumber or an electrician. They wanted a property manager to take care of those problems. The types of people interested in homes for rent are diverse, from millennial couples to people in transition, to retirees looking to downsize their living space.

Because we're always open to new ideas, I watched another company put the concept into action. But we wanted to do it under our name. So, we joined the new world of build-for-rent communities under the umbrella of Everyone's Residence (EVR). It's a mix between single-family housing and duplexes. All the units are for rent but under a single ownership that maintains the grounds and buildings. Our aim is to see that everything is upheld to the highest standards, of course.

Our rental homes are one-, two-, or three-bedroom units with private backyards, dedicated laundry rooms, and spacious primary bedrooms with walk-in closets. Each community has its own common area, with a swimming pool, clubhouse, fitness center, grills for cookouts, and sports courts. Did I mention that each home has a doggie door that leads to the backyard?

We have three EVR communities so far, some within one of our large master-planned communities. Our first was EVR Spur Cross, where homes for rent were built on about 20 acres. They rented almost as soon as they were completed. The second, EVR Porter, on Porter Road in Maricopa, was completed in 2024 and has maintained over 95% occupancy.

## Epilogue: El Dorado Holdings Today

And we're now underway at EVR Bella Vista, where we've set aside 20 acres to build homes for rent. We are looking forward to kicking off a new community in Lubbock, Texas, consisting of duplexes to adapt to its rental market. These communities all offer the benefits of living in a single-family home without the mortgage or maintenance responsibilities that come with home ownership.

As I mentioned earlier, this is just a taste of what El Dorado Holdings has already built or plans to have built. We always have our eyes on new opportunities and future growth. I'm proud of what we've accomplished so far and have no doubt that the younger people running our company now will carry on with our legacy.

My former partner, Monty Ortman (second from the left) with me (on the right) and our architects and contractors onsite during construction of our first golf course community, El Dorado Lakes.

# IN SUMMARY:
# THE ULTIMATE MASTER PLAN

Here's the bottom line: despite my successes—and yes, my failures—I am simply the product of "Small Town America." I was that young kid who struggled to get acceptable grades in school and that kid who was chosen last for every sandlot ballgame. But I was also the kid whose parents taught me a beautiful, simple truth—they loved me. Even though I knew that in my heart, it took many years and many ups-and-downs to fully accept those words. Some of those downs led me to despair.

When I was in the midst of shutting down my companies in Oklahoma, I had serious doubts. The idea of being loved was not on the table then. I had a chief financial officer who had embezzled money, salesmen who fought the sale, and a greedy attorney who tried to get far more than his fair share. I felt let down by many people I'd known and trusted for years. The banks, of course, were no help either. Did I feel loved by anyone? No, not really.

So many times, I could feel darkness closing in on me and questions would tumble through my mind. "How am I going to survive? How am I going to pay the bills? How am I going to make it through this darkness?" During that time, I asked Sheila to leave the bathroom light on at night, even though she likes it pitch black when she's sleeping. She

## In Summary: The Ultimate Master Plan

understood and was gracious about it. She knew I needed to see some ray of light.

And I'm not the only one. I think lots of people in this world need to see a ray of light in their lives, a glimmer of hope. So many people are hurting because they've lost their hope in the world. During that time, I thought long and hard every night in the dark—except for that little bit of light shining from the bathroom. I still leave the light on in the bathroom every night. It's become a habit now. It reminds me that, even in the worst times, hope is always there.

One good thing happened during that dark time. Sheila and I took a trip to Hong Kong. We'd won the trip from one of our suppliers. We believed we'd earned it and thought it could be a good thing for us mentally and emotionally. We flew from Oklahoma City to Seattle, where we stayed overnight at a Howard Johnson's before the long flight to Hong Kong. There was a dinner party for all the other winners that night, but I didn't feel like a party. Sheila went alone. While she was out, I stayed in the room and felt sorry for myself. In fact, I don't believe I've ever sunk so low in depression and despair than I did that night.

Then something unexpected occurred. I turned on the TV to get my mind off my problems. It was Labor Day weekend, and the Jerry Lewis telethon to benefit muscular dystrophy research came on the screen. I didn't change the channel, even though a John Wayne western would have suited me just fine. Instead, I watched Jerry and his "kids." These kids were fighting huge odds against a disease that had paralyzed them.

## In Summary: The Ultimate Master Plan

It gave me a wake-up call. I thought about these kids who would face so much hardship for the rest of their lives, lives that would probably be shortened by their illness. There I sat, healthy and whole, but depressed about my current situation. I was lost in self pity and had no excuse for it.

My wake-up call continued when Sheila got back to the room. She handed me a book she'd picked up, called *The Be (Happy) Attitudes*, by Dr. Robert Schuller, a Christian evangelist and motivational speaker. My attitude changed that night. I started Dr. Schuller's book in the room that night and finished it the next day on the plane. I knew then that a positive attitude had to rule my life.

I learned something else that night. I learned that life is not just about doing good things for others. It's not only about money or investments or even giving. And while our relationships are extremely important, it's not just about that.

Life is about creating a Master Plan for me . . . for you . . . for us. With a lump in my throat, I seriously evaluated Dr. Schuller's thoughts and found my answer. I decided to turn my life around.

Here's what I learned:

> *Life is not all about me. It's about others.*
> *That is the Ultimate Master Plan.*

# A POSTSCRIPT

It's my hope that you'll find something in this book that might inspire you and help you in formulating your own Master Plan. I'd like to leave you with this final thought: Back in the early days of cattle ranches, every rancher had a unique brand to mark his or her herd, to distinguish it from any others. Cowboys who hired on and rode for the brand signaled they were committed and loyal to that rancher. "Ride for the Brand." That phrase was an expression of pride and loyalty for a man's employer or the particular outfit he rode for. It was considered a compliment of the highest order in an almost feudal society. If a man did not like a ranch or the way the rancher conducted affairs, he was free to quit, take his saddle and find another horse it fit—and many did. But if he stayed on, he gave his loyalty and expected to do nothing less.

Red Steagall wrote a poem and song about it called, "Ride for the Brand."

A few years ago, he modified that poem and song. The new version is "I Ride for the Brand of the Man with the Nail Scarred Hands." It definitely is my favorite. Here's an excerpt:

*"I Ride for the Brand of the Man with the Nail Scarred Hands"*
*I saddle up each morning*
*With a grateful heart and mind.*
*I'm happy and my life is so complete.*

## A Postscript

*As I ride through God's Cathedral*
*Where His majesty abounds,*
*I thank Him for his Son who died for me.*

*When I trail the Oreano*
*Into places I've not been,*
*I sometimes feel I'm lost and all alone.*
*But I let my pony have his head*
*And put my trust in him,*
*And like my Lord, he leads me safely home.*

*And though my day be troubled,*
*I will still rise up with joy.*
*I know that I am blessed inside His arms.*
*He told me if I'd follow Him*
*And ride the narrow trail,*
*That He will guide me safely through life's storms.*

*I have pledged my life to Jesus,*
*Feel his power in my soul.*
*I no longer have to fear what I can't see.*
*I feel as though I've sprouted wings,*
*I ride the narrow trail,*
*And strive to be the man He wants of me.*

*And when it comes my time to go,*
*And Jesus calls my name*
*To join the chorus in His angel band,*
*He'll greet me at the Pearly Gates*
*And welcome me inside,*
*'Cause I Ride for the Brand*
*Of the Man with the Nail Scarred Hands.*

# A Postscript

*'Cause I Ride for the Brand*
*Of the Man with the Nail Scarred Hands.*
*I once rode with the devil*
*Through his Hell of burning sand.*
*Then I found the love of Jesus,*
*I was saved and born again.*
*Now I Ride for the Brand*
*Of the Man with the Nail Scarred Hands.*

*Adiós, mis amigos.*
*Red Steagall*

There is an old cowboy saying that is a favorite of Red's and he talks about it in his presentations ... "Be the Man to Ride the River With" ... and he tells it like this: "If you cross the river first, be sure to leave a good horse on the other side." Red's point is to be loyal and trustworthy. "To Red, and any of my other friends, if I cross first, I'll be sure and leave a good horse for you." That's my advice to you. In everything you do in your business, your career, your family, and your faith: Be committed, be loyal and "Ride for the Brand".

WE GO, WE GO NOW. Let's ride.

— Mike Ingram

# A Postscript

### Hats Off to the Cowboy

The city folks think it's all over
That the cowboy has outlived his time
An old worn-out relic, a thing of the past
The truth is he's still in his prime
Hats off to the cowboy, he's still ridin' tall
He's a throwback to days on the trail
He honors his Lord and the man he works for
His saddle is never for sale
His saddle is never for sale
The cowboy's the image of freedom
The hard ridin' boss of the range
His trade is a fair one, he fights for what's right
And his ethics aren't subject to change
Hats off to the cowboy, he's still ridin' tall
Still saddles a rough string with pride
He's a shining example of the life that we love
He's showin' us all how to ride
He's showin' us all how to ride
He still tips his hat to the ladies
Lets you water first at the pond
He believes a day's wages is worth a day's work
And his handshake and word are his bond
Hats off to the cowboy, he's still ridin' tall
He lives by the cow country code
That's respecting your neighbors, your family and friends
And totin' your share of the load
And totin' your share of the load
Hats off to the cowboy, he's still ridin' tall
Don't let him ride out of your sight
'Cause the day he rides off in the sunset alone
Is the day that America dies
Yeah don't let America die

-Red Steagall

One of my very favorite poems and songs of all times: Red Steagall, Western icon— *Hats Off to the Cowboy*.

# ACKNOWLEDGMENTS

Most authors acknowledge the people they love, followed by the people who contributed to the development of their book.

True to form, my first acknowledgment is to my wife, my best friend, and my partner in life, Sheila.

**With my wonderful wife, Sheila, 2024.**

But I obviously owe so much of my success to the people who have partnered with me in business and in life. In fact, I see them as part of the Master Plan for me.

### Acknowledgments

Deb Bricker has been my capable and devoted associate since "day two" in the life of El Dorado Holdings. She has been mentioned several times in this book, but she deserves one more mention here.

Roy McKay and Foster Friess have inspired me from the day I met them—Roy, because he never gives up, and Foster, because he gives and gives.

My amazing mentors have included Virgil Haley, John Tufts, Sr., Dr. Bill Burch, Dr. James Dobson, R.C. "Dick" Cline, Dr. Les Parrott, and Dr. David Le Shana, and of course, Dr. Bill Bright.

**With Dr. James Dobson, author of numerous books on parenting, marriage and faith; host of Family Talk radio program, and founder of Focus on the Family.**

All of my team members, from my wholesale distribution days to my real estate ventures today, have been important people in my life. I especially want to thank Betty Dalton, Sue Ann Dean, David Elcyzyn, Ed Jessup, Sam Holman,

James Walsh, Dal Ward, Nolan Chandler, Sue Buescher, and Denise Organ.

My partners, Monty Ortman, Dr. James Little, John Tufts, Sr., and all of those who have put their trust in me have earned my gratitude.

**With our partners, Crystal Hansen and Mark Victor Hansen. Mark is the Co-Creator and Co-Author of the bestselling book series, *Chicken Soup for the Soul*®.**

Many people have been involved in this book, including Stan Toler, who has offered his invaluable insights for several years; Zig Ziglar, who kept telling me, "You have to write a book;" and Sharon Lechter, who has brought her wisdom and guidance to the project from the perspective of an acclaimed bestselling author and has supported me in updating and revising the original book into this edition. Steve Gottry, who pushed me to focus on the purpose for the book as he crafted my ideas into carefully chosen words that express my heart. My great appreciation goes to Mark

## Acknowledgments

Victor Hansen, also an incredible bestselling author, and his tremendous executive editor, Carol McManus, and lead writer, Veronica Deisler.

A very big thank you to Laura Schwartz for the many hours she spent editing and proofreading. She brought a steady hand, a sharp eye, and a quiet dedication that helped shape these words into the book you're holding now.

And one more time, I want to give thanks to Deb Bricker, my loyal friend and business partner, for over thirty-seven years. Without her, this book would have never happened. And many thanks to you for taking the time to read these words.

# ABOUT THE AUTHOR
# MIKE INGRAM

In 1987, Mike co-founded El Dorado Holdings, Inc., a Phoenix-based land and development company, with Monty Ortman and a total staff of one, Deb Bricker.

Over the years, Mike and El Dorado have faced numerous challenges and economic downturns, but the company has weathered each and every storm and is one of the area's largest private landholding companies, with assets exceeding $1 billion. Mike attributes his success to his faith in God, his ability to surround himself with people smarter than himself, his strong relationships (both business and personal), and his solid belief in the words of his friend and mentor, Zig Ziglar: "You can get everything in life you want, if you help enough other people get what they want."

About the Author

Mike is extremely passionate about giving back to his community and his country. He is committed to a number of business and civic organizations, including the Arizona Commerce Authority, Arizona-Mexico Commission, Barrow Neurological Foundation (emeritus), Translational Genomics Research Institute, C. M. Russell Museum, Shikar Safari Club International, and the National Cowboy & Western Heritage Museum. He is also actively involved with the International Order of T. Roosevelt. Mike's other involvements include the National Rifle Association, the Congressional Sportsmen's Foundation, Safari Club International, the World War II Museum, and the Gary Sinise Foundation. He also served at the pleasure of the secretary of interior on the International Wildlife Conservation Council.

Mike is an avid sportsman who enjoys hunting and fishing in the great outdoors while promoting the North American Model of Wildlife Conservation. A fact that few people are aware of is that funding for most, if not all, of the states' conservation programs, is paid through an excise tax on hunting licenses and associated hunting equipment. The public reaps the benefit of being able to enjoy this country's bountiful wildlife through fees paid by hunters and fishermen. Mike believes we enjoy more wildlife today than ever before in North America, due to the great conservation management programs carried out by the game and fish personnel in every state. He is quick to give thanks to those in the field who serve and protect.

Mike's passion for patriotism is embodied in several of his favorite quotes: from Ronald Reagan, "Freedom is never more than one generation away from extinction;" from

John Quincy Adams, "Children should be educated and instructed in the principles of freedom;" and from Winston Churchill, who modified the original quote from George Santayana to say, "Those who fail to learn from history are condemned to repeat it."

A framed quote by Dr. Robert Schuller hangs near the door of Mike's office. It's titled "The Laminated Principle" and it reads:

> *You Make a Promise—and Deliver.*
> *You Accept an Assignment—and Fulfill It.*
> *You Attempt Something "Impossible"— and Pull it Off.*
> *Finally, year after year, maybe decade after decade, you have applied one accomplishment on top of another, one achievement over another—promises kept, and commitments fulfilled. Your reputation is like a laminated beam that has durability and power. People believe in you. They take you at your word. They'll sign a contract with you because they know you are going to deliver.*

These words have guided Mike Ingram's life. Nothing is more important to Mike than to make the Lord Jesus Christ his first love and to do his best to love and honor Him.

Mike and his wife, Sheila, reside in Paradise Valley, Arizona, and have six children, twenty-one grandchildren, and twenty-one great-grandchildren.

## About the Author

Mounted Shooting fun with "The Wild Gang" — Chris Grogan, Keegan McCarthy, Glenn Stearns, me, Skip Rimsza, and Chelsea McCarthy.

My daily reminder on the dash of my pickup truck from Dr. Bill Bright, asking me the question, "Is Jesus your first love?"

# THE HORATIO ALGER ASSOCIATION

As shared on its website, "The Horatio Alger Association of Distinguished Americans, Inc., a 501(c)(3) nonprofit educational organization, was established in 1947 to dispel the mounting belief among our nation's youth that the American Dream was no longer attainable.

The association bears the name of the renowned author Horatio Alger, Jr., whose tales of overcoming adversity through unyielding perseverance and basic moral principles captivated the public in the late nineteenth century. The organization's founder, Dr. Kenneth Beebe, in close association with Dr. Norman Vincent Peale, hoped to inspire individual Americans to reach their highest potential, thereby strengthening American society as a whole. They created the association to recognize men and women of outstanding achievement as a way to remind Americans of the limitless possibilities that exist through the free-enterprise system.

# The Horatio Alger Association

The Horatio Alger Association of Distinguished Americans is dedicated to the simple but powerful belief that hard work, honesty, and determination can conquer all obstacles. The Association honors the achievements of outstanding leaders who have accomplished remarkable successes despite adversity by bestowing upon them the Horatio Alger Award and inducting them as lifetime members. Since 1947, more than 800 distinguished individuals from all walks of life and diverse professional backgrounds have received the Horatio Alger Award and lifetime membership in the Association. There are currently over 300 living members, including members from Canada.

Horatio Alger members support promising young people with the resources and confidence needed to overcome adversity and pursue their dreams through higher education. Thanks to its generosity, in 2018, the Association awarded more than $16 million in undergraduate and graduate need-based scholarships across the United States and Canada and provided college support and mentoring services to its scholars. Since 1984, the Association has awarded more than $275 million in college scholarships to more than 38,000 deserving young people.

For more Information about the Horatio Alger Society visit: https://horatioalger.org/

In recognition of his life's work and dedication to others, Mike Ingram was a 2019 recipient of the Horatio Alger Award. He was presented with the award and inducted as a lifetime member of the Horatio Alger Association at a special induction ceremony during a three-day celebration held in Washington, D.C., from April 4 to 6, 2019.

## The Horatio Alger Association

Mike is honored and proud to join the distinguished recipients of the Horatio Alger Award, including many of his friends, such as Foster Friess, Glenn Stearns, John Elway, Reba McEntire, Dennis Washington, Mark Victor Hansen, Michael Shannon, Harvey Mackay, John Grundhofer, Larry Ruvo, Tom Brokaw, Harold Hamm, T. Denny Sanford, R.C. Slocum, Matthew Rose, T. Boone Pickens, John Maxwell, Marcia Taylor, Justice Clarence Thomas, Roger Staubach, and many more.

Philanthropist, retired Super Bowl winning quarterback for the Denver Broncos, and an El Dorado Holdings partner, John Elway, with one of my cow dog pups.

www.ingramcontent.com/pod-product-compliance
Lightning Source LLC
Chambersburg PA
CBHW041313240426
43669CB00024B/2974